W9-APX-132

Academic
Learning
Series

Microsoft®
SQL Server™ 2000
System Administration

Lab Manual

Microsoft®

PUBLISHED BY
Microsoft Press
A Division of Microsoft Corporation
One Microsoft Way
Redmond, Washington 98052-6399

Library of Congress Cataloging-in-Publication Data
    MCSE Training Kit: Microsoft SQL Server 2000 System Administration / Microsoft Corporation.
        p. cm.
    Includes index.
    ISBN 0-7356-1247-1
    ISBN 0-7356-1426-1 (Academic Learning Series)
    ISBN 0-07-285076-0 (McGraw-Hill Ryerson)
    1. Electronic data processing personnel--Certification.   2. Microsoft
software--Examinations--Study guides.   3. SQL server.   I. Title.

    QA76.3 .R32   2001
    005.75'85--dc21   2001016231

Printed and bound in the United States of America.

1 2 3 4 5 6 7 8 9   QWT   8 7 6 5 4 3

Distributed by McGraw-Hill Ryerson.

A CIP catalogue record for this book is available from the British Library.

Microsoft Press books are available through booksellers and distributors worldwide. For further information about international editions, contact your local Microsoft Corporation office or contact Microsoft Press International directly at fax (425) 936-7329. Visit our Web site at mspress.microsoft.com. Send comments to tkinput@microsoft.com.

FrontPage, Microsoft, Microsoft Press, Outlook, PowerPoint, Visual Basic, Visual C++, Windows, and Windows NT are either registered trademarks or trademarks of Microsoft Corporation in the United States and/or other countries. Other product and company names mentioned herein may be the trademarks of their respective owners.

The example companies, organizations, products, domain names, e-mail addresses, logos, people, places, and events depicted herein are fictitious. No association with any real company, organization, product, domain name, e-mail address, logo, person, place, or event is intended or should be inferred.

Acquisitions Editor: Thomas Pohlmann
Project Editor: Melissa von Tschudi-Sutton
Technical Editor: L.J. Locher
Manuscript Editor: Roger LeBlanc
Desktop Publishers: Gina Cassill, Jean Trenary

Author: Carl Rabeler

SubAssy Part No. X09-56871
Body Part No. 097-0003610

Introduction

This Lab Manual supplements the *ALS: Microsoft SQL Server 2000 System Administration* textbook. The labs in this manual are designed to be performed in a classroom environment by a group of students under the supervision of an instructor. This is in contrast to the exercises in the textbook, which are designed to be performed outside the classroom. The labs in this manual and the exercises in the textbook are an essential part of your training. The opportunity to explore the menus, options, and responses will ensure an understanding of the appropriate use of SQL Server 2000.

The labs in this manual do not precisely mirror the exercises in the textbook. Domain names, user names, IP addresses, shared resources, and other specific references in this manual are different than those in the textbook. Also, because each institution's local networking requirements are unique, there might be slight differences between the names and addresses in your classroom and those appearing in these labs. Your instructor will explain any differences.

The labs in this manual are performed in a classroom that is configured as an isolated network. The instructor computer is a Microsoft Windows 2000 domain controller in the Contoso.msft domain. Each student computer is a member server in the Contoso.msft domain. The lab files required for this course have been copied to the C:\Labfiles folder.

The Microsoft Certified Professional (MCP) exams are demanding in both the knowledge and the hands-on experience they require. Students preparing for the Microsoft certification tests can increase their competence by gaining firsthand experience in the implementation and management of SQL Server 2000. One of the best ways to become confident in the use of SQL Server 2000 is to complete all the assigned labs in this manual as well as the exercises in the textbook.

Lab 1: Installing Microsoft SQL Server 2000

Objectives

After completing this lab, you will be able to

- Use the SQL Server 2000 Setup program
- Perform an interactive installation of SQL Server 2000
- Perform an unattended installation of SQL Server 2000
- Review the SQL Server error log using Notepad

Before You Begin

Each computer in the classroom is running Microsoft Windows 2000 Advanced Server and is a member of the Contoso.msft domain. The instructor computer is the domain controller of this domain and is running Active Directory directory services, Domain Name System (DNS), and Dynamic Host Configuration Protocol (DHCP). Each student computer is named Server*xx*, where *xx* is a two-digit number between 01 and 12. For each student, there is a domain user account, Student*xx*, that corresponds to each student computer. For example, the domain user account for Server01 is Student01. This domain user account is also a member of the local Administrators group on that computer.

Note You must log on to your student computer using the correct domain user account to have sufficient permissions to perform the lab exercises in this Lab Manual.

Estimated time to complete this lab: 45 minutes

Exercise 1
Performing an Interactive Installation of SQL Server 2000

In this exercise, you will use the SQL Server 2000 Setup program to perform an interactive setup of the default instance of SQL Server 2000 on your local computer.

▶ **To log on to Windows 2000 and start the SQL Server 2000 Setup program**

1. Press Ctrl+Alt+Del to log on to the Contoso.msft domain.

   The Log On To Windows dialog box appears.

2. Verify that the User Name text box displays Student*xx* (where *xx* is your computer number).

3. Verify that the Log On To drop-down list displays Contoso. (If the Log On To drop-down list does not appear, click the Options button.)

4. In the Password text box, type **password** and then click OK.

   Personal settings are applied, and you are logged on to Windows 2000. The Microsoft Windows 2000 Configure Your Server wizard appears.

5. Clear the Show This Screen At Startup check box, and then close the Microsoft Windows 2000 Configure Your Server wizard.

6. Insert the Microsoft SQL Server 2000 Evaluation Edition compact disc into the CD-ROM drive.

   The Microsoft SQL Server 2000 Evaluation Edition screen appears.

7. Click SQL Server 2000 Components, and then, on the Install Components screen, click Install Database Server.

   The Welcome To The Microsoft SQL Server Installation Wizard page appears.

▶ **To install client and server tools for the default instance of SQL Server 2000**

1. Click Next to begin installing SQL Server 2000.

   The Computer Name page appears.

2. Verify that the Local Computer option button is selected, and then click Next.

   The Installation Selection page appears.

3. Verify that the Create A New Instance Of SQL Server, Or Install Client Tools option button is selected, and then click Next.

   The User Information page appears.

4. Type your name in the Name text box, and then click Next.

   The Software License Agreement page appears, displaying the 120-day Evaluation License for Microsoft SQL Server 2000.

5. Click the Yes button to accept the terms of the license agreement.

   The Installation Definition page appears.

6. Verify that the Server And Client Tools option button is selected, and then click Next.

   The Instance Name page appears.

7. Verify that the Default check box is selected, and then click Next.

   The Setup Type page appears.

▶ **To perform a typical setup of SQL Server 2000**

1. Verify that the Typical option button is selected, and then click Next.

   The Services Accounts page appears.

2. Click the Customize The Settings For Each Service option button.

3. In the Services group box, verify that the SQL Server option button is selected.

4. In the Service Settings group box, verify that the Use A Domain User Account option button is selected.

5. In the Service Settings group box, type **SQLService** in the Username text box and **sql** in the Password text box.

6. In the Service Settings group box, verify that Contoso appears in the Domain text box.

7. In the Service Settings group box, select the Auto Start Service check box.

8. In the Services group box, click the SQL Server Agent option button.

9. In the Service Settings group box, type **SQLService** in the Username text box and **sql** in the Password text box.

10. In the Service Settings group box, verify that Contoso appears in the Domain text box.

11. In the Service Settings group box, select the Auto Start Service check box.

    A Setup message box appears stating there is a dependency between SQL Server and the SQL Server Agent Services, which assures that SQL Server is running whenever Agent Services is started.

12. Click OK, and then click Next on the Services Accounts page.

    The Authentication Mode page appears.

13. Verify that the Windows Authentication Mode option button is selected, and then click Next.

    The Start Copying Files page appears.

14. Click Next.

    The SQL Server 2000 Setup program begins installing SQL Server 2000, beginning with the Microsoft Data Access Components (MDAC). When the SQL Server 2000 Setup program is complete, the Setup Complete page appears.

15. Click the Finish button.

Exercise 2
Performing an Unattended Installation of SQL Server 2000

In this exercise, you will use the SQL Server 2000 Setup program to create unattended installation files and then perform an unattended installation of SQL
Server 2000 using these files.

▶   **To create unattended installation files using the SQL Server 2000 Setup
program**

1. On the desktop, double-click the My Computer icon.

   The My Computer window appears.

2. Double-click your CD-ROM drive icon (which will be displaying the
   SQL2000_Eval label).

   The Microsoft SQL Server 2000 Evaluation Edition screen appears.

3. Click SQL Server 2000 Components, and then, on the Install Components
   screen, click Install Database Server.

   The Welcome To The Microsoft SQL Server Installation Wizard page appears.

4. Click Next.

   The Computer Name page appears.

5. Verify that the Local Computer option button is selected, and then click Next.

   The Installation Selection page appears.

6. Click the Advanced Options option button, and then click Next.

   The Advanced Options page appears.

7. Verify that the Record Unattended .ISS File option button is selected, and
   then click Next.

   The User Information page appears.

▶   **To record installation options in the Setup.iss file**

1. On the User Information page, type your name in the Name text box, and then
   click Next.

   The Software License Agreement page appears, displaying the 120-day
   Evaluation License for Microsoft SQL Server 2000.

2. Click the Yes button to accept the terms of the license agreement.

   The Installation Definition page appears.

3. Verify that the Server And Client Tools option button is selected, and then
   click Next.

   The Instance Name page appears.

4. In the Instance Name text box, type **Instance2** and then click Next.

   The Setup Type page appears.

5. Verify that the Typical option button is selected and then click Next.

   The Services Accounts page appears.

6. Verify that the Use The Same Account For Each Service. Auto Start SQL Server Service. option button is selected.

7. In the Service Settings group box, type **SQLService** in the Username text box and **sql** in the Password text box.

8. In the Service Settings group box, verify that Contoso appears in the Domain text box.

9. Click OK, and then click Next.

   The Authentication Mode page appears.

10. Verify that the Windows Authentication Mode option button is selected, and then click Next.

    The Setup Information page appears.

11. Click Next.

    The Setup Complete page appears.

12. Click the Finish button.

▶ **To run the unattended installation batch file using the Setup.iss file to install SQL Server 2000**

1. Using Windows Explorer, locate the Setup.iss file in C:\Winnt.

2. Right-click Setup.iss, and then click Open With.

   A Caution dialog box appears to warn you that you are attempting to open an Unattended Setup File (.ISS) and that editing it could damage your system.

3. Click the Open With button.

   The Open With dialog box appears.

4. Click Notepad, and then click OK.

5. Review the entries in the .ISS file.

6. Right-click the Windows 2000 taskbar, and then click Task Manager.

   The Windows Task Manager dialog box appears.

7. Click the Performance tab to observe the CPU Usage and MEM Usage bar graphs during the installation.

8. Click Start, and then click Run.

   The Run dialog box appears.

9. In the Open drop-down combo box, type the following command (for the –f argument, use the number "1" not the letter "l"):

```
e:\x86\setup\setupsql.exe k=SMS -s -m -SMS -f1 "c:\winnt\setup.iss"
```

Note You must type this command exactly or the unattended installation will fail. The paths in this command assume that your CD-ROM drive is E: and that your Windows 2000 installation is C:\Winnt. If your paths are different, change the path names accordingly.

10. Click OK.

An unattended installation of a named instance of SQL Server 2000 commences. Setup should take no more than 5 or 10 minutes. Watch the CPU Usage History graph to verify that the installation is continuing. If the CPU Usage History graph indicates that CPU usage returns to a low number quickly, you have probably typed the batch command incorrectly.

Note You can verify that both instances have been installed by checking SQL Server Enterprise Manager. You do this by clicking Start, pointing to Programs, pointing to Microsoft SQL Server, clicking Enterprise Manager, and then expanding the Microsoft SQL Servers and SQL Server Group containers. Both of the instances should be listed in the console tree.

11. Close the Windows Task Manager dialog box when setup is complete.

12. Close Notepad and all open windows.

Exercise 3
Reviewing the SQL Server Error Log

In this exercise, you will review the SQL Server error log to become familiar with the type of information recorded in these logs.

▶ **To locate the SQL Server error log files and configure Windows Explorer**

1. Click Start, point to Search, and then click For Files Or Folders.

   The Search Results window appears.

2. In the Search For Files Or Folders Named text box, type **Errorlog** and then click the Search Now button.

   Two items appear in the Search Results pane.

   Why are two SQL Server error log files found with the same name?

   _____

   _____

3. On the View menu, click Details.

   The items in the Search Results pane now display all file details. You can now determine the appropriate SQL Server error log file for each instance based on the full path.

   What is the full path for the SQL Server error log for the named instance?

   _____

4. On the Tools menu, click Folder Options.

   The Folder Options dialog box appears with the General tab selected.

5. Click the View tab.

6. In the Advanced Settings list box, clear the Hide File Extensions For Known File Types check box.

7. Select the Display The Full Path In The Address Bar check box.

8. Select the Display The Full Path In The Title Bar check box.

9. In the Folder Views group box, click the Like Current Folder button.

   A Folder Views dialog box appears, asking for confirmation that you want to make this change.

10. Click the Yes button.

11. Click OK to close the Folder Options dialog box.

▶   **To open and review the SQL Server error logs for each instance using Notepad**

1. In the Search Results pane, right-click the SQL Server error log file for the default instance and then click Open With.

    The Open With dialog box appears.

2. Click Notepad, and then click OK.

    The contents of the current error log for the default instance appear in Notepad.

3. Switch to the Search Results dialog box.

4. Right-click the SQL Server error log file for the named instance, and then click Open With.

    The Open With dialog box appears.

5. Click Notepad, and then click OK.

    The contents of the current error log for the named instance appear in Notepad.

6. Close the Search Results dialog box.

7. Verify that the only two open windows on your desktop are the two Notepad windows. Right-click the Windows taskbar, and then click Tile Windows Horizontally.

    The two Notepad windows are tiled horizontally on your desktop. Review the entries related to the startup of SQL Server 2000 for each instance. List the four primary differences between the startup of each instance.

    _____

    _____

    _____

    _____

8. Close both instances of Notepad.

9. Log off of your computer.

Lab 2: Preparing to Use Microsoft SQL Server 2000

Objectives

After completing this lab, you will be able to

- Review NTFS and registry permissions related to Microsoft SQL Server 2000
- Start SQL Server services using the SQL Server Service Manager and the NET command
- Connect to and query SQL Server 2000 using Osql and SQL Query Analyzer
- Configure SQL Server Enterprise Manager

Before You Begin

You must successfully complete Exercises 1 and 2 in Lab 1 before you begin this lab.

Note You must log on to your student computer using the correct domain user account to have sufficient permissions to perform the lab exercises in this Lab Manual. Your Student*xx* account is a member of the local Administrators group on your computer.

Estimated time to complete this lab: 60 minutes

Exercise 1
Reviewing Installed Folders and Permission Settings

In this exercise, you will use Windows Explorer and Windows Registry Editor to review permissions set by the SQL Server Setup program during the installation of SQL Server 2000.

▶ **To review SQL Server 2000 folders using Windows Explorer**

1. Press Ctrl+Alt+Del to log on to the Contoso.msft domain.

   The Log On To Windows screen appears.

2. Verify that the User Name text box displays Student*xx* (where *xx* is your computer number).

3. Verify that the Log On To drop-down list displays Contoso. (If the Log On To drop-down list does not appear, click the Options button.)

4. In the Password text box, type **password** and then click OK.

   Personal settings are applied, and you are logged on to Windows 2000.

5. Click Start, point to Programs, point to Accessories, and then click Windows Explorer.

   The Windows Explorer window appears.

6. In the console tree, expand My Computer, expand Local Disk (C:), expand Program Files, and then expand Microsoft SQL Server.

   Notice that there are three subfolders, named 80, Mssql, and Mssql$Instance2.

   Briefly describe the differences between the types of files contained in each of these three subfolders.

   _____

   _____

   _____

7. In the console tree, expand C:\Program Files\Microsoft SQL Server\80, expand Tools, and then click Binn.

8. In the details pane, click the Type column to sort the contents of the Binn folder by type of file.

   How many client management tools does the SQL Server Setup program install in this Binn folder?

   _____

   _____

9. In the console tree, expand C:\Program Files\Microsoft SQL Server\Mssql and then click Binn.

10. In the details pane, click the Type column to sort the contents of the Binn folder by type of file.

How many client management tools does the SQL Server Setup program install in this Binn folder?

_____

Briefly explain the difference between the client management tools installed in this Binn folder and the client management tools installed in the Binn folder you looked at in Step 8 above.

_____

_____

_____

11. In the console tree, expand C:\Program Files\Microsoft SQL Server\Mssql$Instance2 and then click Binn.

12. In the details pane, click the Type column to sort the contents of the Binn folder by type of file.

Are the client management tools that are installed in this Binn folder the same tools that are installed for the default instance?

_____

▶ **To review NTFS permissions on the installed folders**

1. In the console tree, right-click the C:\Program Files folder and then click Properties.

The Local Disk (C:) Properties dialog box appears with the General tab selected.

2. Click the Security tab.

Review the users with permissions on this folder.

3. Click Cancel to close the Local Disk (C:) Properties dialog box.

4. In the console tree, right-click the C:\Program Files\Microsoft SQL Server\80 folder and then click Properties.

The 80 Properties dialog box appears with the General tab selected.

5. Click the Security tab.

Review the users with permissions on this folder. Notice that this common SQL Server folder inherits its permissions from its parent folder.

6. Click Cancel to close the 80 Properties dialog box.

7. In the console tree, right-click the C:\Program Files\Microsoft SQL Server\80\Tools\Binn folder and then click Properties.

The Binn Properties dialog box appears with the General tab selected.

8. Click the Security tab.

    Review the users with permissions on this folder. Notice that this common SQL Server folder inherits its permissions from its parent folder.

    Can any authenticated user within the Contoso.msft domain execute any client administration tool in the C:\Program Files\Microsoft SQL Server\80\Tools\Binn folder?

    _____

9. Click Cancel to close the Binn Properties dialog box.

10. In the console tree, right-click the C:\Program Files\Microsoft SQL Server\Mssql folder and then click Properties.

    The Mssql Properties dialog box appears with the General tab selected.

11. Click the Security tab.

    Review the users with permissions on this folder.

    Can any authenticated user within the Contoso.msft domain execute any client administration tool in the C:\Program Files\Microsoft SQL Server\Mssql\Binn folder?

    _____

12. Click Cancel to close the Binn Properties dialog box.

13. Close Windows Explorer.

▶   **To review permissions on registry keys**

1. Click Start, and then click Run.

    The Run dialog box appears.

2. In the Open drop-down combo box, type **regedt32** and then click OK.

    The Registry Editor appears.

3. Maximize the Registry Editor window.

4. Maximize the HKEY_LOCAL_MACHINE On Local Machine window.

5. In the console tree for the HKEY_LOCAL_MACHINE On Local Machine window, expand SOFTWARE, expand Microsoft, expand Microsoft SQL Server, and then click 80.

    This key is common to the default and all named instances. This key relates to the shared files.

6. On the Security menu, click Permissions.

    The Permissions For 80 dialog box appears. Notice that the user permissions on this registry key are essentially the same as the NTFS permissions for the C:\Program Files\Microsoft SQL Server\80 folder.

7. Click Cancel to close the Permissions For 80 dialog box.

8. In the console tree, click INSTANCE2.

   This key relates to the unique program and data files for your named instance.

9. On the Security menu, click Permissions.

   The Permissions For Instance2 dialog box appears. The permissions on this registry key are essentially the same as the NTFS permissions for the C:\Program Files\Microsoft SQL Server\Mssql$Instance2 folder.

10. Click Cancel to close the Permissions For Instance2 dialog box.

11. Expand the INSTANCE2 key.

    Notice the subkeys under this key.

12. Click the MSSQLServer subkey under the INSTANCE2 key.

13. On the Security menu, click Permissions.

    The Permissions For MSSQLServer dialog box appears. Notice that the permissions for this subkey are inherited from the parent key.

14. Click Cancel to close the Permissions For MSSQLServer dialog box.

15. In the console tree, collapse the Microsoft SQL Server key.

16. In the console tree, expand SOFTWARE\Microsoft\MSSQLServer.

    Notice the subkeys under this key. Notice an additional subkey for this key, the Client key. This subkey contains client connection information for all instances and has different permission settings than the other subkeys under this key.

17. Click the Providers subkey under the MSSQLServer key.

18. On the Security menu, click Permissions.

    The Permissions For Providers dialog box appears. Notice that the permissions for this subkey are not inherited from the parent key. Because of the different structure of the MSSQLServer key, all subkeys must have security set individually.

19. Click Cancel to close the Permissions For Providers dialog box.

20. In the console tree under SOFTWARE\Microsoft, expand Windows NT, expand CurrentVersion, and then click Perflib.

21. On the Security menu, click Permissions.

    The Permissions For Perflib dialog box appears. Notice that the SQLService domain user account has been given Full Control permission on this registry key. This permission is required for performance condition alerts to work properly.

22. Click Cancel to close the Permissions For Perflib dialog box.

23. In the console tree under SOFTWARE, expand Clients, and then click Mail.

24. On the Security menu, click Permissions.

The Permissions For Mail dialog box appears. Notice that the SQLService domain user account has been given Full Control permission on this registry key. This permission is required for SQL Mail and SQLAgentMail to work properly.

25. Click Cancel to close the Permissions For Mail dialog box.
26. Close the Registry Editor.

Exercise 2
Starting SQL Server Services

In this exercise, you will learn how to use the SQL Server Service Manager and the NET command to start the SQL Server services.

▶ **To open SQL Server Service Manager and start the SQL Server service for the default instance**

1. Click Start, point to Programs, point to Microsoft SQL Server, and then click Service Manager.

   The SQL Server Service Manager dialog box appears. In the Server drop-down combo box, Server*xx* (where *xx* represents your server number) appears. In the Services drop-down list, SQL Server appears.

2. Click the Start/Continue button (green triangle) to start the SQL Server service.

   Note If you have rebooted your computer since you performed Lab 1, it will already be running.

   The status line indicates that the SQL Server service on your computer is starting, and then indicates that it is running. Also, the server display changes the red square to a green arrow to indicate the applicable service is running.

3. In the Services drop-down list, change the displayed service to SQL Server Agent.

   The dialog box changes to display the status of the SQL Server Agent service. Notice that this service is configured to start automatically because the Auto-Start Service When OS Starts check box is selected, and that the status line indicates this service is stopped (unless you have rebooted your computer). Notice also that the icon in the system tray changes slightly to indicate the SQL Server Agent service rather than the SQL Server service.

4. In the Server drop-down combo box, change the server to display Server*xx*\Instance2 (where *xx* represents your computer number).

   The dialog box changes to display the status of the SQL Server Agent service for Instance2. Notice that this service is not configured to start automatically, and that the status line indicates this service is stopped.

   Why is the SQL Server Agent service configured to start automatically for the default instance but not for Instance2?

5. In the Services drop-down list, change the displayed service to SQL Server.

   The dialog box changes to display the status of the SQL Server service for Instance2. Notice that this service is configured to start automatically and that the status line indicates this service is stopped (unless you have rebooted your computer).

6. Close the SQL Server Service Manager dialog box.

Notice that the SQL Server Service Manager icon remains in the system tray on the taskbar (in the lower right-hand corner). Also notice that it is displaying the status of the SQL Server service for Instance2. Finally, notice that it displays a pulse every five seconds, which indicates the frequency with which it is verifying the current status of that service.

▶ **To open a command prompt and use the NET command to start the SQL Server service for Instance2**

1. Click Start, point to Programs, point to Accessories, and then click Command Prompt.

The Command Prompt window appears.

2. In the Command Prompt window, type **net start** and then press Enter.

A list of all Windows 2000 services that have started is displayed. Notice that MSSQLServer has started. Notice that the Distributed Transaction Coordinator and Microsoft Search services have also started.

3. Type **net start sqlagent$instance2** and then press Enter.

Notice that the SQL Server Agent service for your named instance starts. The SQL Server service is also started because the SQL Server Agent service requires the SQL Server service to also be running. Finally, notice that the SQL Server Service Manager icon on the taskbar indicates that the SQL Server service for this instance has started.

4. In the Command Prompt window, type **net start** and then press Enter.

Notice that MSSQL$Instance2 and SQLAgent$Instance2 have both started. Also, notice the SQL Server Service Manager indicates the SQL Server service is now running for Instance2.

5. In the Command Prompt window, type **net stop sqlagent$instance2** and then press Enter.

Notice that only the SQL Server Agent service stops.

6. Do not close the Command Prompt window.

Exercise 3
Connecting To and Querying SQL Server Instances

In this exercise, you will use the Osql command-prompt utility and the SQL Query Analyzer graphical tool to connect to the default instance and to Instance2. You will also query the system databases using Osql and SQL Query Analyzer.

▶ **To connect to and query SQL Server 2000 instances using Osql**

1. In the Command Prompt window, type **OSQL –E** and then press Enter.

   Osql connects to the default instance of SQL Server 2000 on your local server (Server*xx*) and then displays a 1> prompt, waiting for more input from you. If you cannot connect, you will receive an Open Database Connectivity (ODBC) error message. Typing a lowercase "e" rather than an uppercase "E" is a frequent error.

Note You can connect to each instance on your computer because you are a local administrator. By default, members of the local Administrators group on a computer are system administrators on all SQL Server instances on that computer. See Chapters 10 and 11 for more information on SQL Server 2000 security.

---

2. At the 1> prompt, type **SELECT @@SERVERNAME** and then press Enter to query the SQL Server 2000 default instance using the @@SERVERNAME configuration function.

   Notice that the 2> prompt appears.

   Why was the SELECT statement not executed when you pressed the Enter key?

---

3. At the 2> prompt, type **SELECT @@VERSION** and then press Enter to query the SQL Server 2000 default instance using the @@VERSION configuration function.

   Notice that the 3> prompt appears and that neither command is executed.

4. At the 3> prompt, type **GO** and then press Enter to submit the batch to SQL Server 2000 for processing.

   SQL Server 2000 is queried and returns the name of your local server (Server*xx*) and the version (including the edition) of SQL Server (Microsoft SQL Server 2000, Enterprise Evaluation Edition) that is installed on your computer. In addition, the version of your Windows operating system is displayed. It also returns you to a 1> prompt for a new query.

5. Type **EXIT** and then press Enter.

   Osql exits and returns you to the command prompt.

6. In the Command Prompt window, type **OSQL –L** and then press Enter.

   Executing Osql using the –L argument returns the names of each of the instances of SQL Server that are installed on your local computer and broadcasting on your network (including each instance on each student computer in the classroom).

Important This next step requires you to work with a partner. You will need to work with this same partner for all partner exercises in this Lab Manual. Your partner's computer will always be referred to as Server*yy*, where the variable *yy* represents your partner's computer number.

---

7. At the prompt, type **OSQL –E –S Server*yy*** (you must replace the variable *yy* with the number of your partner's computer) and then press Enter.

   Notice that you cannot establish a connection to your partner's default instance.

   Why are you unable to connect to your partner's default instance?

---

8. At the prompt, type **OSQL –E –S Server*xx*\Instance2** (you must replace the variable *xx* with the number of your computer) and then press Enter.

   Osql connects to Instance2 of SQL Server 2000 on your computer and then displays a 1> prompt, waiting for more input from you.

9. At the >1 prompt, type **SELECT SYSTEM_USER** and then press Enter.

   SYSTEM_USER is a niladic function used to return the current system username.

10. Type **GO** and then press Enter.

    Osql returns your current security context within SQL Server 2000. Because you connected to SQL Server 2000 using a trusted connection, your current security context is Contoso\Student*xx*. Osql then displays a 1> prompt, waiting for more input from you.

11. Type **QUIT** and then press Enter.

12. Close the Command Prompt window.

▶ **To connect to and query SQL Server 2000 instances using SQL Query Analyzer**

1. Click Start, point to Programs, point to Microsoft SQL Server, and then click Query Analyzer.

   SQL Query Analyzer appears displaying the Connect To SQL Server dialog box with no information displayed in the SQL Server drop-down combo box.

2. Verify that the Windows Authentication option button is selected, and then click OK to connect to the default instance on your computer using Windows authentication.

   You are connected to the default instance of SQL Server 2000 on your computer using your Windows user account. Verify this by reviewing the active query window title bar.

3. Press the F8 key to toggle the Object Browser. Leave the Object Browser visible.

4. In the query pane, type **SELECT * FROM INFORMATION_SCHEMA .SCHEMATA** and then click the Execute Query button on the toolbar. (You can also press either F5 or Ctrl+E.)

   This query uses information schema views to query this instance of SQL Server 2000 for all databases in this instance. Information schema views will be covered in Chapter 5. Notice the color coding. Blue indicates a keyword, and gray indicates an operator. Refer to the "Color Coding in SQL Query Analyzer" topic in SQL Server Books Online for more information regarding color coding. Notice that the result set from the query is displayed in the Results pane in the form of a grid. How many databases did the SQL Server Setup program install?

   _____

5. In the Object Browser, expand Master and then expand Views.

6. Right-click INFORMATION_SCHEMA.SCHEMATA, and then click Open.

   The Open Table window appears. Notice that the Open Table window displays the same information as the previous query.

7. Close the Open Table window.

8. In the results pane of the original query, click the Messages tab.

   An informational message regarding the number of rows affected by the query ("6 row(s) affected") is displayed.

9. In the query pane, select INFORMATION_SCHEMA.SCHEMATA and then press Shift+F1.

   SQL Server Books Online appears with INFORMATION_SCHEMA.SCHEMATA highlighted in the console tree.

10. In the SQL Server Books Online console tree, double-click INFORMATION_SCHEMA.SCHEMATA View and then review the information in the details pane for Schemata.

11. Close SQL Server Books Online.

12. In the query pane of SQL Query Analyzer, type **SELECT @@SERVERNAME** on a new line.

Notice that the color of @ @SERVERNAME changed to magenta when SQL Query Analyzer recognized this character string.

13. Select this new query only, and then press Ctrl+E to execute just this query.

    Notice that you can select and execute a single query in a query window. The name of your server (Serverxx) is returned.

14. On the toolbar, click the Clear Window button. (You can also press Ctrl+Shift+Del.)

    The contents of the query pane are erased.

15. On the toolbar, click the Show Results Pane button. (You can also press Ctrl+R.)

    This toggles the results pane, hiding the results pane.

16. Press Ctrl+R.

    This toggles the results pane again, restoring the results pane to visibility.

17. On the toolbar, click the New Query button. (You can also press Ctrl+N.)

    A new query window appears. Compare the two query panes. Notice that you are connected to the same database in the same instance of SQL Server 2000 using the same security context.

18. In the active query window, type **USE Northwind** and then click the Execute Query button to execute the query.

    Notice that the current database displayed on the toolbar changed to Northwind. Also notice that the active query window title bar now indicates a connection to the Northwind database rather than the master database.

19. On the File menu, click Connect.

    The Connect To SQL Server dialog box appears.

20. Next to the SQL Server drop-down combo box, click the ellipsis (…) button, select Serverxx\Instance2 (where xx represents your computer number), and then click OK.

    Notice that this named instance now appears in the SQL Server drop-down combo box.

21. Verify that the Windows Authentication option button is selected, and then click OK to connect to your named instance.

    A new query window appears. The title bar indicates that you are connected to the master database in your named instance. Notice that the current data-base on the toolbar is master.

22. Close SQL Query Analyzer.

    A SQL Query Analyzer message box appears.

23. Click the No To All button. Do not save any queries.

Exercise 4
Configuring SQL Server Enterprise Manager

In this exercise, you will configure the SQL Server Enterprise Manager Microsoft Management Console (MMC). You will add the Event Viewer snap-in and review default registration information.

▶ **To add the Event Viewer snap-in to the SQL Server Enterprise Manager MMC**

1. Click Start, point to Programs, point to Microsoft SQL Server, and then click Enterprise Manager.

   SQL Server Enterprise Manager appears, displaying the Microsoft SQL Servers console tree in the console root. No other console trees appear.

2. On the MMC toolbar, click Console.

   Notice that the only option available is Exit. No other menu options are available because the SQL Server Enterprise Manager MMC was configured to open in user mode.

3. Click Exit to close SQL Server Enterprise Manager.

4. Click Start, point to Search, and then click For Files Or Folders.

   The Search Results dialog box appears.

5. In the Search For Files Or Folders Named text box, type ***.msc** and then click the Search Now button.

   Notice that a plethora of preconfigured MMC consoles appear. Most are separate MMC consoles, each for specific Windows 2000 administrative tasks.

6. Right-click SQL Server Enterprise Manager.msc, and then click Author.

   The SQL Server Enterprise Manager MMC console appears in author mode.

7. On the MMC toolbar, click Console and then click Add/Remove Snap-In.

   The Add/Remove Snap-In dialog box appears.

8. Click the Add button.

   The Add Standalone Snap-In dialog box appears, displaying all the available standalone snap-ins that can be added.

9. Select Event Viewer, and then click the Add button.

   The Select Computer dialog box appears.

10. Click the Finish button to accept the default configuration, which is to always manage the local computer.

11. Click the Close button to close the Add Standalone Snap-In dialog box, and then click OK to close the Add/Remove Snap-In dialog box.

    The SQL Server Enterprise Manager MMC console now displays two separate console trees, Microsoft SQL Servers and Event Viewer (Local).

12. On the Console menu, click Exit.

A Microsoft Management Console dialog box appears.

13. Click the Yes button to save these new console settings to the default SQL Server Enterprise Manager MMC console.

14. Close the Search Results dialog box.

15. Click Start, point to Programs, point to Microsoft SQL Server, and then click Enterprise Manager.

SQL Server Enterprise Manager appears displaying the Microsoft SQL Servers and the Event Viewer (Local) console trees in the console root.

16. Click the Event Viewer (Local) console tree container.

The logs available within Event Viewer appear in the details pane. Notice that the menu items and tools on the console root toolbar change when you change console trees. The console root title bar indicates your focus within the console root.

17. Click the Microsoft SQL Servers console tree container.

Notice that the menu items and tools on the console root toolbar specific to SQL Server Enterprise Manager appear in place of the items on the Event Viewer toolbar. Also notice that the contents of the details pane change based on your focus in the console tree.

18. Expand the Microsoft SQL Servers container, and then expand the SQL Server Group container.

Your default instance (Server*xx*) and your named instance (Server*xx*\Instance2) appear in the Microsoft SQL Servers console tree, each in its own container and displaying the state of the SQL Server service for that instance. Each instance also displays the authentication method used to connect to the instance, enclosed in parentheses (namely Windows authentication).

Note If the named instance is not registered, right-click SQL Server Group and then click New SQL Server Registration. Follow the instructions in the wizard to complete the registration. You can tell that the named instance is not registered when the container for that instance is not listed in the Microsoft SQL Servers console tree.

Notice that your focus in the console tree remains the Microsoft SQL Servers container and that the contents of the details pane do not change when you expand an item in the console tree. The details pane changes only when your focus changes (by clicking on an item in the console tree).

19. Click the container for your default instance (Server*xx*, where *xx* represents your computer number).

Notice that the details pane displays the contents of this container. We will cover each of these objects in detail throughout the course of this book. Also notice that the icon indicating the state of the SQL Server service changed from a green triangle in a white circle to a white triangle in a green circle. This indicates that you have established a connection to this instance.

20. On the SQL Server Enterprise Manager toolbar, click the View menu.

    Notice the available options, including Taskpad. The container object that is your current focus contains a preconfigured view.

21. Click Taskpad.

    Notice that the details pane changes to display the taskpad view for this container object. The taskpad contains two tabs, General and Wizards. The General tab displays information regarding your computer and your server configuration. The Wizards tab displays the wizards that are available for your use. These wizards are also available from the Tools menu. We will use these wizards in exercises in later chapters of this book.

22. In the Microsoft SQL Servers console tree, right-click the container for your default instance and then click Edit SQL Server Registration Properties.

    The Registered SQL Server Properties dialog appears. Notice the configured registration properties.

23. Click Cancel.

24. Close SQL Server Enterprise Manager.

25. Log off of your computer.

Lab 3: Viewing Data File and Transaction Log File Properties

Objectives

After completing this lab, you will be able to

- View the properties of a data file
- View the properties of a transaction log file
- View the recovery model used by a database
- View the database compatibility level

Before You Begin

You must successfully complete Exercises 1 and 2 in Lab 1 before you begin this lab.

Note You must log on to your student computer using the correct domain user account to have sufficient permissions to perform the lab exercises in this Lab Manual.

Estimated time to complete this lab: 15 minutes

Exercise 1
Viewing the Properties of Database Files

In this exercise, you will use SQL Server Enterprise Manager to view the properties of Microsoft SQL Server 2000 data and transaction log files.

▶   **To view the properties of a data file**

1. Press Ctrl+Alt+Del to log on to the Contoso.msft domain.

   The Log On To Windows screen appears.

2. Verify that the User Name text box displays Student*xx* (where *xx* is your computer number).

3. Verify that the Log On To text box displays Contoso. (If the Log On To text box does not appear, click the Options button.)

4. In the Password text box, type **password** and then click OK.

   Personal settings are applied, and you are logged onto Microsoft Windows 2000.

5. Click Start, point to Programs, point to Microsoft SQL Server, and then click Enterprise Manager.

   SQL Server Enterprise Manager appears, displaying the Microsoft SQL Servers and the Event Viewer (Local) console trees in the console root.

6. In the console tree, expand the Microsoft SQL Servers container, expand the SQL Server Group container, expand the Server*xx* container (the default instance), and then expand the Databases container.

7. In the console tree, right-click msdb and then click Properties.

   The Msdb Properties dialog box appears with the General tab selected, displaying various properties of the msdb database, such as the database status, date of last backup, and collation name.

   What is the current size for the msdb database?

   _____

   _____

8. Click the Data Files tab.

   What is the current size of the data file for the msdb database?

   _____

   What is the logical name of the data file for the msdb database?

   _____

   What is the physical name of the data file for the msdb database?

   _____

List three other properties of the msdb data file that are displayed.

_____

_____

▶ **To view the properties of a transaction log file**

1. Click the Transaction Log tab.

    What is the current size of the transaction log file for the msdb database?

    _____

    _____

    What is the logical name of the transaction log file for the msdb database?

    _____

    What is the physical name of the transaction log file for the msdb database?

    _____

    List three other properties of the msdb transaction file that are displayed.

    _____

    _____

▶ **To view the recovery model and database compatibility level used for the msdb database**

1. Click the Options tab.

    What is the recovery model used for the msdb database?

    _____

    What is the database compatibility level used for the msdb database?

    _____

2. Click Cancel to close the Msdb Properties dialog box.

3. Review the properties of each of the other system databases by right-clicking them and then clicking Properties.

    Do any of the system databases use a recovery model other than Simple Recovery?

    _____

4. Click Cancel to close the Msdb Properties dialog box.

5. Close SQL Server Enterprise Manager.

Exercise 2
Querying System Tables

In this exercise, you will learn how to query system tables using a number of different methods. These include Transact-SQL statements, system stored procedures, system functions, and information schema views.

▶ **To query system tables directly using Transact-SQL statements**

1. Click Start, point to Programs, point to Microsoft SQL Server, and then click Query Analyzer.

   SQL Query Analyzer appears, displaying the Connect To SQL Server dialog box.

2. Verify that the Windows Authentication option button is selected, and then click OK to connect to your default instance using Windows authentication.

   SQL Query Analyzer appears, displaying a new query window.

3. Press F8 to hide the Object Browser, and then expand the query pane.

4. In the query pane, type **SELECT * FROM sysdatabases** and then click the Execute Query button on the toolbar.

   Notice that the results pane displays information regarding each database in this instance of SQL Server 2000.

5. On the toolbar, click the Clear Window button (or press Ctrl+Shift+Del simultaneously).

6. In the query pane, type **SELECT * FROM sysaltfiles** and then click the Execute Query button on the toolbar.

   Notice that the results pane displays information regarding each data and transaction log file used by this instance of SQL Server 2000.

   What is the size of the data file for the msdb database (reported as the number of 8 KB pages)?

   _____

   What is the size of the transaction log file for the msdb database (reported as the number of 8 KB pages)?

   _____

7. On the toolbar, click the Clear Window button (or press Ctrl+Shift+Del simultaneously).

▶ **To query system tables using system stored procedures**

1. In the SQL Query Analyzer query pane, type **sp_helpdb**.

2. On the toolbar, click the Execute Query button.

   Notice that the results pane displays information regarding each database in this instance of SQL Server 2000.

3. In the query pane, type a space and then **Northwind** to modify your query to read sp_helpdb Northwind.

4. On the toolbar, click the Execute Query button.

   Notice that the results pane displays information regarding the Northwind database only, including an additional result set showing the file allocation for the Northwind database.

5. On the toolbar, click the Clear Window button.

6. In the query pane, type **sp_spaceused**.

7. On the toolbar, click the Execute Query button.

   Notice that the results pane displays information regarding space used by the current database (in this case, master).

8. On the toolbar, click the drop-down list and then change the current database to msdb.

9. On the toolbar, click the Execute Query button.

   Notice that the results pane displays information regarding space used by the current database, which is now msdb.

   What amount of space in the data file is used for data in the msdb database? What is the remaining space used for?

   _____

   _____

   _____

10. On the toolbar, click the drop-down list and then change the current database to Northwind.

11. In the query pane, type **'customers'** to modify your query to read sp_spaceused 'customers' and then click the Execute Query button on the toolbar.

    Notice that the results pane now displays information regarding space used by the Customers table in the Northwind database. Notice that the index uses more space than the actual data in the Customers table.

12. On the toolbar, click the Clear Window button.

▶ **To query system tables using system functions**

1. In the SQL Query Analyzer query pane, type **SELECT DB_ID ('Northwind')**.

2. On the toolbar, click the Execute Query button.

   Notice that the results pane displays the database ID for the Northwind database in this instance of SQL Server 2000. Also notice that only a single value is retrieved. This enables the value returned by a system function to be used programmatically.

3. On the toolbar, click the Clear Window button.

4. In the query pane, type **SELECT FILEPROPERTY ('Northwind', 'SpaceUsed')** and then click the Execute Query button on the toolbar.

   Notice that the results pane displays the number of pages allocated in the Northwind database.

5. On the toolbar, click the Clear Window button.

6. In the query pane, type **SELECT USER_NAME (2)** and then click the Execute Query button on the toolbar.

   Notice that the results pane displays the name for the user with a user ID of 2. (This is the Guest account.)

7. On the toolbar, click the Clear Window button.

▶ **To query system tables using information schema views**

1. In the SQL Query Analyzer query pane, type **SELECT * FROM INFORMATION_SCHEMA.SCHEMATA** and then click the Execute Query button on the toolbar.

   Notice that the results pane displays information regarding all databases in this instance of SQL Server 2000.

2. On the toolbar, click the Clear Window button.

3. In the query pane, type **SELECT * FROM INFORMATION_SCHEMA.TABLES** and then click the Execute Query button on the toolbar.

   Notice that the results pane displays information regarding tables in the current database.

4. On the toolbar, click the Clear Window button.

5. In the query pane, type **SELECT * FROM INFORMATION_SCHEMA.TABLE_PRIVILEGES** and then click the Execute Query button on the toolbar.

   Notice that the results pane displays information regarding privileges on all tables in the Northwind database.

6. Close SQL Query Analyzer.

   A SQL Query Analyzer dialog box appears, asking whether you want to save the changes in the query pane.

7. Click the No button.

8. Log off of your computer.

Lab 4: Creating and Working with Databases

Objectives

After completing this lab, you will be able to

- Create a database using the Create Database wizard
- Create a database using Microsoft SQL Server Enterprise Manager directly
- Create a database using the CREATE DATABASE Transact-SQL statement
- Script an existing database using SQL Server Enterprise Manager
- Modify database properties using SQL Server Enterprise Manager
- Detach and reattach a database

Before You Begin

You must have successfully completed Exercises 1 and 2 in Lab 1 before you begin this lab.

Note You must log on to your student computer using the correct domain user account to have sufficient permissions to perform the lab exercises in this Lab Manual.

Estimated time to complete this lab: 75 minutes

Exercise 1
Creating a Database Using the Create Database Wizard in SQL Server Enterprise Manager

In this exercise, you create a database using the Create Database wizard in the SQL Server Enterprise Manager.

▶ **To start the Create Database wizard**

1. Press Ctrl+Alt+Del to log on to the Contoso.msft domain.

   The Log On To Windows screen appears.

2. Verify that the User Name text box displays Student*xx* (where *xx* is your computer number).

3. Verify that the Log On To text box displays Contoso. (If the Log On To text box does not appear, click the Options button.)

4. In the Password text box, type **password** and then click OK.

   Personal settings are applied, and you are logged on to Microsoft Windows 2000.

5. Click Start, point to Programs, point to Microsoft SQL Server, and then click Enterprise Manager.

   SQL Server Enterprise Manager appears displaying the Microsoft SQL Servers and the Event Viewer (Local) console trees in the console root.

6. In the console tree, expand the Microsoft SQL Servers container, expand the SQL Server Group container, expand the Server*xx* container (the default instance), and then click the Databases container.

7. On the Tools menu, click Wizards.

   The Select Wizard dialog box appears.

8. Expand Database, and then double-click Create Database Wizard.

   The Welcome To The Create Database Wizard screen appears.

▶ **To create a database using the Create Database wizard**

1. In the Welcome To The Create Database Wizard page, click Next.

   The Name The Database And Specify Its Location page appears.

2. In the Database Name text box, type **DB_1**.

3. In the Transaction Log File Location text box, type **D:** and then click Next.

Note If drive D isn't the second partition or drive that your instructor has formatted on your computer, replace D:\ with the correct drive letter of your second partition or drive.

The Name The Database Files page appears. Notice the default primary data file name and default initial size for the primary data file. When you use the Create Database wizard, both the logical filename and the physical filename are the same for each data file. Also notice that you can add data files, but only in the default location.

4. In the Initial Size (MB) cell, type **5**, and then click Next.

The Define The Database File Growth page appears. Notice the default settings.

5. In the Grow The Files By Percent: spin box, type **25**.

6. Click the Restrict File Growth To MB: option button, and then in the Restrict File Growth To MB: spin box, type **30**.

7. Click Next.

The Name The Transaction Log Files page appears. Notice the default name and initial size. The default initial size is the same size as the default initial data file size.

8. In the Initial Size (MB) cell, type **5** and then click Next.

The Define The Transaction Log File Growth page appears.

9. Click the Grow The Files In Megabytes (MB): option button, and then in the Grow The Files In Megabytes (MB): spin box, type **5**.

10. Click the Restrict File Growth To MB: option button, and then in the Restrict File Growth To MB: spin box, type **20**.

11. Click Next.

The Completing The Create Database Wizard page appears.

12. Click the Finish button.

A Create Database Wizard message box appears letting you know that the database was successfully completed.

13. Click OK.

A Create Database Wizard dialog box appears asking whether you want to create a maintenance plan for this database.

14. Click the No button.

▶ **To review database properties of the DB_1 database**

1. In the SQL Server Enterprise Manager console tree, expand the Databases container for your default instance.

Notice that the DB_1 database appears in the list of databases.

2. Right-click DB_1, and then click Properties.

The DB_1 Properties dialog box appears with the General tab selected.

3. Click the Data Files tab, and then review the properties of the data file for the DB_1 database.

4. Click the Transaction Log tab, and then review the properties of the transaction log file for the DB_1 database.

5. Click Cancel to close the DB_1 Properties dialog box.

6. Do not close SQL Server Enterprise Manager.

Exercise 2
Creating a Database Using SQL Server Enterprise Manager Directly

In this exercise, you will create a database directly using SQL Server Enterprise Manager.

▶ **To create a database directly using SQL Server Enterprise Manager**

1. In the SQL Server Enterprise Manager console tree, right-click the Databases container for the default instance and then click New Database.

   The Database Properties dialog box appears with the General tab selected.

2. In the Name text box, type **DB_2**.

   Notice that this new database inherits the default collation.

3. Click the Data Files tab.

   Notice the default logical filename, physical name and location, initial size, filegroup, and file growth properties.

4. In the File Name column, overwrite the default primary file name by typing **DB_2_Data1** in the first cell of the column.

   Notice that the physical filename in the corresponding Location cell changes to DB_2_Data1_Data.mdf.

5. In the corresponding Initial Size (MB) cell for the primary data file, type **10**.

6. In the File Growth group box, type **15** in the By Percent: spin box.

7. In the Maximum File Size group box, click the Restrict File Growth (MB): option button, and then in the Restrict File Growth (MB): spin box, type **25**.

8. In the File Name column, click the cell in the second line and then type **DB_2_Data2**.

   Notice the default parameters for this new data file. In particular, notice in the Location cell that the default name for this secondary data file ends with the .NDF suffix.

9. Change the physical location for this secondary data file to D:\DB_2_Data2_Data.ndf.

Note If drive D isn't the second partition or drive that your instructor has formatted on your computer, substitute D:\ with the correct drive letter of your second partition or drive.

---

10. In the corresponding Initial Size (MB) cell, type **50**.

11. In the File Growth group box, type **15** in the By Percent: spin box.

12. In the Maximum File Size group box, click the Restrict File Growth (MB): option button, and then in the Restrict File Growth (MB): spin box, type **100**.

13. Click the Transaction Log tab.

    Notice the default parameters for this new transaction log file. On a production system, you would not generally have a data file and a transaction log file sharing the same drive.

14. In the Initial Size (MB) cell, type **20** to replace the default parameter.

15. In the File Growth group box, type **25** in the By Percent: spin box.

16. In the Maximum File Size group box, click the Restrict File Growth (MB): option button, and then in the Restrict File Growth (MB): spin box, type **50**.

17. Click OK to create the new database.

▶   **To review database properties of the DB_2 database**

1. In the SQL Server Enterprise Manager console tree, verify that the Databases container is expanded for the default instance.

   Notice that the DB_2 database appears in the list of databases.

2. Right-click DB_2, and then click Properties.

   The DB_2 Properties dialog box appears, with the General tab selected.

3. Click the Data Files tab and review the properties of the data files for the DB_2 database.

4. Click the Transaction Log tab, and review the properties of the transaction log file for the DB_2 database.

5. Click Cancel to close the DB_2 Properties dialog box.

6. Do not close SQL Server Enterprise Manager.

Exercise 3
Creating a Database Using the CREATE DATABASE Statement

In this exercise, you will create a database using the CREATE DATABASE statement in SQL Query Analyzer.

▶ **To create a database using the CREATE DATABASE statement**

1. On the SQL Server Enterprise Manager Tools menu, click SQL Query Analyzer.

   SQL Query Analyzer appears. A connection is automatically established to the default instance using your Student*xx* user account.

2. On the toolbar, click the Load SQL Script button or press Ctrl+Shift+P.

   The Open Query File dialog box appears.

3. Browse to the C:\Labfiles\Lab 6 folder, and then open the CreateDB.sql script.

Note Paths in the CreateDB.sql script assume that your second partition or drive is drive D and that SQL Server 2000 is installed on drive C. If your paths are different, change the pathnames in the script accordingly.

---

4. Review this script, which is shown below.

```
CREATE DATABASE DB_3
ON
( NAME = DB_3_DATA ,

FILENAME = 'C:\Program Files\Microsoft SQL Server\Mssql\Data\DB_3_data.mdf' ,
 SIZE = 10 ,
 MAXSIZE = 25 ,
 FILEGROWTH = 5 )
LOG ON
( NAME = DB_3_LOG ,
 FILENAME = 'D:\DB_3_log.ldf' ,
 SIZE = 4 ,
 MAXSIZE = 12 ,
 FILEGROWTH = 40% )
```

5. On the toolbar, click the Execute Query button to execute the CreateDB.sql script.

   Notice that the results pane displays the results of the creation of the DB_3 database. The DB_3_Data file was allocated 10 MB, and the DB_3_Log file was allocated 4 MB.

6. On the toolbar, click the Clear Window button.

7. In the query pane, type **EXEC sp_helpdb DB_3** and then press Ctrl+E (to execute the query) on your keyboard.

8. Review the output in the results pane to verify the properties of the DB_3 database.

9. Close SQL Query Analyzer. Do not save any changes.

10. Do not close SQL Server Enterprise Manager.

Exercise 4
Generating a Transact-SQL Script to Re-Create the DB_1 Database

In this exercise, you will use SQL Server Enterprise Manager to generate a Transact-SQL script to re-create the DB_1 Database.

▶ **To generate a Transact-SQL script to re-create the DB_1 database**

1. In the SQL Server Enterprise Manager console tree, verify that the Databases container for the default instance is expanded, right-click DB_1, point to All Tasks, and then click Generate SQL Script.

   The Generate SQL Scripts – Server*xx*\DB_1 dialog box appears with the General tab selected.

2. Click the Options tab.

3. In the Security Scripting Options group box, select the Script Database check box and then click OK.

   The Save As dialog box appears, with the My Documents folder as the save location.

4. In the File Name text box, type **DB_1** and then click the Save button.

   A Scripting message box appears.

5. Click OK to close the Scripting message box.

▶ **To review and test the DB_1 script**

1. In the SQL Server Enterprise Manager console tree, expand Server*xx*\Instance2 (the named instance), and then click the Databases container.

   In the details pane, notice that there is no DB_1 database in this SQL Server instance.

2. On the Tools menu, click SQL Query Analyzer.

   SQL Query Analyzer appears. A connection is automatically established to the named instance using your Student*xx* user account. The connection was made to the named instance because it was your focus within SQL Server Enterprise Manager.

3. On the toolbar, click the Load SQL Script button.

   The Open Query File dialog box appears with the My Documents folder as the default location.

4. Open the DB_1.sql script.

   Notice that the script begins with a DROP DATABASE Transact-SQL statement and a CREATE DATABASE Transact-SQL statement. Notice also that it contains the database option settings for the DB_1 database.

5. On the Edit menu, click Replace.

   The Replace dialog box appears.

6. In the Find text box, type **DB_1_Data.mdf**.

7. In the Replace With text box, type **DB_1_Data2.mdf**.

8. Click the Replace All button.

   This eliminates the duplicate physical file name for the primary data file. You could also change the location of the data and log files from the default instance location to the named instance location, but this is not necessary.

9. In the Find text box, type **DB_1_Log.ldf**.

10. In the Replace With text box, type **DB_1_Log2.ldf**.

11. Click the Replace All button.

    This eliminates the duplicate physical file name for the transaction log file.

12. Click Cancel.

13. On the toolbar, click the Execute Query button.

    A database identical to DB_1 in the default SQL Server instance is created in the named instance.

14. Close SQL Query Analyzer.

    A SQL Query Analyzer dialog box appears asking whether you want to save changes.

15. Click the Yes button to save the changes.

16. In the SQL Server Enterprise Manager console tree, right-click the Databases container for the named instance and then click Refresh.

    Notice that DB_1 appears in the details pane.

17. Right-click DB_1, and then click Properties.

    The DB_1 Properties dialog box appears with the General tab selected. Verify that the properties of this database are identical (other than different physical file names) to the DB_1 database in the default instance.

18. Click Cancel to close the DB_1 Properties dialog box.

19. Do not close SQL Server Enterprise Manager.

Exercise 5
Modifying Data and Transaction Log File Properties

In this exercise, you will use SQL Server Enterprise Manager to modify data and transaction log file properties.

► **To modify autogrowth settings for the DB_1 database**

1. In the SQL Server Enterprise Manager console tree, expand the Databases container for the named instance, right-click DB_1, and then click Properties.

   The DB_1 Properties dialog box appears with the General tab selected, displaying various properties of the DB_1 database.

2. Click the Data Files tab.

   Notice that the primary data file for the DB_1 database has an initial size of 5 MB, is set to grow automatically in 25 percent increments, and has a maximum size of 30 MB.

3. In the Space Allocated (MB) cell, type **25**.

4. Clear the Automatically Grow File check box.

5. Click the Transaction Log tab.

   Notice that the transaction log file for the DB_1 database has an initial size of 5 MB, is set to grow automatically in 5 MB increments, and has a maximum size of 20 MB.

6. In the Space Allocated (MB) cell, type **10**.

7. Clear the Automatically Grow File check box.

8. Click OK to apply these changes to the DB_1 database.

Exercise 6
Detaching and Reattaching a Database

In this exercise, you will use SQL Server Enterprise Manager to detach the DB_2 database from the default instance and then attach it to the named instance.

▶ **To detach a database**

1. In the SQL Server Enterprise Manager console tree, verify that the Databases container is expanded for the default instance.

2. Right-click DB_2, point to All Tasks, and then click Detach Database.

   The Detach Database – DB_2 dialog box appears. Notice that there are no connections using this database and that the database is not being replicated.

3. Click OK to detach the database.

   A SQL Server Enterprise Manager message box appears to inform you that the database has detached successfully.

4. Click OK to close the SQL Server Enterprise Manager message box.

   Notice that the DB_2 database no longer appears in the Databases container for the default instance.

▶ **To attach a database**

1. In the SQL Server Enterprise Manager console tree, verify that the Databases container is expanded for the named instance.

2. Right-click Databases, point to All Tasks, and then click Attach Database.

   The Attach Database – Server*xx*\Instance2 dialog box appears.

3. Click the ellipsis button to search for the .MDF file for the DB_2 database.

   The Browse For Existing File – Server*xx*\Instance2 dialog box appears.

4. Expand C:\, expand the Program Files folder, expand the Microsoft SQL Server folder, expand the Mssql folder, and then expand the Data folder.

5. Click the DB_2_Data1_Data.mdf file, and then click OK.

   In the Attach Database – Server*xx*\Instance2 dialog box, notice that the primary data file and the transaction log file are located successfully (as indicated by the green check). However, the secondary data file is not located because it is not located in the default location (as indicated by the red x).

6. In the Current File(s) Location cell for the DB_2_Data2_Data.ndf file, type **D:\DB_2_Data2_Data.ndf,** and then click the Attach As text box.

   Notice that the check box for the secondary data file now has a green check indicating that SQL Server is now ready to attach all required files for this database.

7. In the Attach As text box, type **DB_2_Attached**.

8. In the Specify Database Owner drop-down list, click sa.

9. Click OK to attach the DB_2 database with a new database name.

   A SQL Server Enterprise Manager message box appears, informing you that the database has attached successfully.

10. Click OK to close the SQL Server Enterprise Manager message box.

    Notice that the DB_2_Attached database appears in the Databases container for the named instance.

11. Close SQL Server Enterprise Manager.

12. Log off of your computer.

Lab 5: Populating a Database

Objectives

After completing this lab, you will be able to

- Import and transform data using the DTS Import/Export wizard
- Create and edit DTS packages using DTS Designer
- Add DTS connections to a DTS package
- Add DTS tasks using DTS Designer
- Create workflow constraints using DTS Designer
- Modify data using an ActiveX script in a DTS package
- Save DTS packages using multiple formats
- Import data using Bcp
- Import data using the BULK INSERT statement

Before You Begin

You must have successfully completed Exercises 1 and 2 in Lab 1 before you begin this lab.

Note You must log on to your student computer using the correct domain user account to have sufficient permissions to perform the lab exercises in this Lab Manual.

Estimated time to complete this lab: 75 minutes

Exercise 1
Transferring and Transforming Data Using the DTS Import/Export Wizard

In this exercise, you transfer and transform data using the DTS Import/Export wizard. First you transfer tables from one database to another. Second, you use a Transact-SQL query to transform data being transferred from a table in one database to a table in another database.

▶ **To start the DTS Import/Export wizard**

1. Press Ctrl+Alt+Del to log on to the Contoso.msft domain.

   The Log On To Windows screen appears.

2. Verify that the User Name text box displays Student*xx* (where *xx* is your computer number).

3. Verify that the Log On To text box displays Contoso. (If the Log On To text box does not appear, click the Options button.)

4. In the Password text box, type **password** and then click OK.

   Personal settings are applied and you are logged on to Microsoft Windows 2000.

5. Click Start, point to Programs, point to Microsoft SQL Server, and then click Enterprise Manager.

   SQL Server Enterprise Manager appears displaying the Microsoft SQL Servers and Event Viewer (Local) console trees in the console root.

6. In the console tree, expand the Microsoft SQL Servers container, expand the SQL Server Group container, and then click the Server*xx* container (the default instance).

7. Click View. If taskpad isn't selected, click Taskpad.

   The Server*xx* taskpad view appears in the details pane.

8. In the details pane, click the Wizards tab.

   Links to various wizards appear.

9. Under Setup A Database, click Import Data.

   The Data Transformation Services Import/Export Wizard page appears.

▶ **To select a data source and a data destination**

1. In the Data Transformation Services Import/Export Wizard page, click Next.

   The Choose A Data Source page appears.

2. In the Data Source drop-down list, verify that the selected data source is Microsoft OLE DB Provider For SQL Server.

3. In the Server drop-down list, select Server*xx*\Instance2 (the named instance).

4. Verify that the Use Windows Authentication option button is selected.

5. In the Database drop-down list, select Northwind and then click Next.

   The Choose A Destination page appears.

6. In the Destination drop-down list, verify that the selected data destination is Microsoft OLE DB Provider For SQL Server.

7. In the Server drop-down list, select Server*xx* (where *xx* is your computer number).

8. Verify that the Use Windows Authentication option button is selected.

9. In the Database drop-down list, select <New>.

   The Create Database dialog box appears.

10. In the Name text box, type **ReportsDB** and then click OK.

    The Choose A Destination page reappears displaying the new database in the Database drop-down list.

▶ **To specify the data to import and review the transformations**

1. Click Next.

   The Specify Table Copy Or Query page appears.

2. Verify that the Copy Table(s) And View(s) From The Source Database option button is selected and then click Next.

   The Select Source Tables And Views page appears.

3. Click the Select All button.

   Notice that the wizard automatically fills in the name for each destination table that uses the same name as the source table.

4. Click the Transform ellipsis button for the Categories table.

   The Column Mappings And Transformations dialog box appears displaying the details of the new destination Categories table that will be created in the destination database based on the meta data of the source table.

5. Click the Transformations tab.

   Notice that the default transformation is to simply copy each source column directly to the destination column without any transformations.

6. Click Cancel.

7. In the Select Source Tables And Views page, click Next.

   The Save, Schedule, And Replicate Package page appears.

▶ **To save and run the DTS package**

1. Verify that the Run Immediately check box is selected.

2. Select the Save DTS Package check box, verify that the SQL Server option button is selected, and then click Next.

   The Save DTS Package page appears.

3. In the Name text box, type **NwindReports**.

4. In the Owner Password text box, type **OwnerPass**.

5. In the User Password text box, type **UserPass**.

6. In the Server Name drop-down list, select Server*xx* (where *xx* is your computer number).

7. Verify that the Use Windows Authentication option button is selected, and then click Next.

   The Completing The DTS Import/Export Wizard page appears.

8. Click the Finish button.

   The Executing Package dialog box appears displaying the status of the package execution, showing each step. When the package finishes executing, a DTS Import/Export Wizard message box appears stating that 29 tables were successfully copied from Microsoft SQL Server to Microsoft SQL Server.

9. Click OK.

10. On the Executing Package page, briefly review the successfully completed steps and then click the Done button.

▶ **To choose a data source and a data destination for a new package**

1. In the SQL Server Enterprise Manager console tree, expand the Server*xx* container, right-click the Databases container and then click Refresh.

2. Expand the Databases container for the default instance.

3. Right-click ReportsDB, point to All Tasks, and then click Import Data.

   The Data Transformation Services Import/Export Wizard page appears.

4. Click Next.

   The Choose A Data Source page appears.

5. In the Data Source drop-down list, verify that the selected data source is Microsoft OLE DB Provider For SQL Server.

6. In the Server drop-down list, select Server*xx*\Instance2 (where *xx* is your computer number).

7. Verify that the Use Windows Authentication option button is selected.

8. In the Database drop-down list, select Northwind and then click Next.

   The Choose A Destination page appears.

9. In the Destination drop-down list, verify that the selected data destination is Microsoft OLE DB Provider For SQL Server.

10. In the Server drop-down list, verify that Server*xx* (where *xx* is your computer number) is selected.

11. Verify that the Use Windows Authentication option button is selected.

12. In the Database drop-down list, verify that ReportsDB is selected and then click Next.

    The Specify Table Copy Or Query page appears.

▶ **To use a query to filter and summary data to import**

1. Click the Use A Query To Specify The Data To Transfer option button, and then click Next.

   The Type SQL Statement page appears.

2. Click the Browse button.

   The Open dialog box appears.

3. Using the Look In drop-down list, browse to C:\Labfiles\Lab 7 and open the Query.sql script.

Note If your \Labfiles folder isn't stored on drive C, replace C:\ with the correct drive letter.

The contents of the Query.sql script appear in the Query Statement text box.

4. Click Next.

   The Select Source Tables And Views page appears.

5. Click the Results cell in the Destination column, and type **ProductsList**.

   Make sure you type ProductsList as a single word with no spaces.

6. Click the Preview button.

   The View Data dialog box appears displaying the results of the query.

7. Click OK.

   The Select Source Tables And Views page reappears.

8. Click the ellipsis button in the Transform column.

   The Column Mappings And Transformations dialog box appears.

9. Click the Edit SQL button.

   The Create Table SQL Statement dialog box appears.

10. Review the Transact-SQL statement.

    Notice that the ListUnitPrice column allows nulls.

11. Click OK to close the Create Table SQL Statement dialog box.

    The Column Mappings And Transformations dialog box reappears.

12. In the Mappings grid, clear the Nullable check box for the row displaying the ListUnitPrice column.

13. Click the Edit SQL button to review the Transact-SQL statement.

    The Create Table SQL Statement dialog box appears. Notice that the ListUnitPrice column no longer allows nulls.

14. Click OK to close the Create Table SQL Statement dialog box.

15. Click OK to close the Column Mappings And Transformations dialog box.

 The Select Source Tables And Views page reappears.

▶ **To save and run the DTS package**

1. Click Next.

 The Save, Schedule, And Replicate Package page appears.

2. Verify that the Run Immediately check box is selected.

3. Select the Save DTS Package check box.

4. Click the SQL Server Meta Data Services option button, and then click Next.

 The Save DTS Package page appears.

5. In the Name text box, type **Products List**.

6. In the Server Name drop-down list box, click Server*xx* (where *xx* is your computer number).

7. Verify that the Use Windows Authentication option button is selected and then click Next.

 The Completing The DTS Import/Export Wizard page appears.

8. Click the Finish button.

 The Executing Package dialog box appears displaying the status of the package execution, showing each step. When the package finishes executing, a DTS Import/Export Wizard message box appears stating that one table was successfully copied from Microsoft SQL Server to Microsoft SQL Server.

9. Click OK.

10. Briefly review the successfully completed steps in the Executing Package dialog box, and then click the Done button.

11. In the SQL Server Enterprise Manager console tree, expand the ReportsDB container within the Databases container for the default instance, and then click the Tables container.

12. Right-click Tables, and then click Refresh.

13. In the details pane, right-click ProductsList, point to Open Table, and then click Return All Rows.

 The Data In Table 'ProductsList' In 'ReportsDB' On 'Server*xx*' window appears displaying the contents of this newly created and populated table.

14. Close the Data In Table 'ProductsList' In 'ReportsDB' On 'Server*xx*' window.

15. Do not close SQL Server Enterprise Manager.

Exercise 2
Editing and Modifying a DTS Package in DTS Designer

In this exercise, you will edit the DTS package you created in Exercise 1 and add elements to the package.

▶ **To open and review the properties of an existing DTS package in DTS Designer**

1. In the SQL Server Enterprise Manager console tree, expand the Data Transformation Services container for the default instance and then click the Meta Data Services Packages container.

   The details pane displays the Products List DTS package.

2. In the details pane, double-click Products List.

   The DTS Designer window appears displaying the Products List DTS package. Notice two connections and a CREATE TABLE task.

3. Maximize the DTS Designer window, right-click the Connection 1 icon and then click Properties.

   The Connection Properties dialog box appears. Notice that this is the connection to the Northwind database on the named instance.

4. Click Cancel.

5. Right-click the Connection 2 icon, and then click Properties.

   The Connection Properties dialog box appears. Notice that this is the connection to the ReportsDB database on the default instance.

6. Click Cancel.

7. Right-click the black data transformation arrow between the Connection 1 icon and the Connection 2 icon, and then click Properties.

   The Transform Data Task Properties dialog box appears and displays the transforming Transact-SQL query.

8. Click Cancel.

9. Right-click the Create Table ProductsList Step icon, and then click Properties.

   The Execute SQL Task Properties dialog appears and displays the CREATE TABLE Transact-SQL statement. Also notice that this DTS task uses Connection 2.

10. Click Cancel.

11. Right-click the blue stripe workflow arrow between the Create Table ProductsList Step icon and the Connection 1 icon, and then click Properties.

    The Workflow Properties dialog box appears displaying the precedence constraint between the Create Table ProductsList Step (the source step) and the Copy Data From Results To ProductsList Step (the destination step).

12. Click Cancel.

▶ **To add a DROP TABLE step to this DTS package**

1. On the Task menu, click Execute SQL Task.

   The Execute SQL Task Properties dialog box appears.

2. In the Description text box, type **Drop Table ProductsList Step**.

3. In the Existing Connection drop-down list, click Connection 2.

4. In the SQL Statement text box, type the following Transact-SQL statement.

   ```
   DROP TABLE ReportsDB.dbo.ProductsList
   ```

5. Click the Parse Query button to verify that you have typed the Transact-SQL statement correctly.

   A DTS Designer message box appears informing you that the statement parsed successfully.

6. Click OK.

7. Click OK to close the Execute SQL Task Properties dialog box.

8. In the DTS Designer workspace, move the Drop Table ProductsList Step icon so that it is next to the Create Table ProductsList Step icon.

9. Verify that the Drop Table ProductsList Step icon is selected, and then press Ctrl on your keyboard and click the Create Table ProductsList Step icon.

   Notice that both steps are now selected.

10. Right-click either step, point to Workflow and then click On Completion.

11. Right-click the blue workflow arrow between the Create Table ProductsList Task icon and the Connection 1 icon, and then click Properties.

    The Workflow Properties dialog box appears.

12. In the Precedence column, select the Success constraint from the drop-down list and then click OK.

13. On the toolbar, click the Execute button.

    The Executing DTS Package: Products List dialog box appears displaying the progress of the package execution. When the package execution has completed, a Package Execution Results message box appears.

14. Click OK.

    Review the Executing DTS Package: ProductsList dialog box. Notice that each of the three steps completed successfully.

15. Click the Done button.

16. On the toolbar, click the Save button.

▶ **To add a text file connection to this DTS package**

1. On the toolbar, click the Zoom button and then click 100%.

2. From the Connection tool palette, drag the Text File (Source) icon to an open area of the workspace.

The Connection Properties dialog box appears.

3. Verify that the New Connection option button is selected and then, in the New Connection text box, type **Shippers Text File**.

4. In the File Name text box, type **C:\Labfiles\Lab 7\Shippers.txt**.

Note If your \Labfiles folder isn't stored on drive C, replace C:\ with the correct drive letter.

---

5. Click OK.

   A Text File Properties dialog box appears displaying the Select File Format page. Notice the default file format parameters and the preview of the content of the text file.

6. Select the First Row Has Column Names check box, and then click Next.

   A Text File Properties dialog box appears displaying the Specify Column Delimiter page.

7. Verify that the Comma option button is selected for the delimiter type, and then click the Finish button.

   The Connection Properties dialog box reappears.

8. Click OK.

   Notice that the Shippers Text File icon appears in the workspace.

▶ **To add and define a data transformation step for the shipper data**

1. Verify that the Shippers Text File icon is selected, and then press the Ctrl key on your keyboard and click the Connection 2 icon.

   Notice that both icons are now selected.

2. Right-click either highlighted icon, and then click Transform Data Task.

   A black data transformation arrow appears between the two icons, pointing to the Connection 2 icon.

3. Right-click the new data transformation arrow, and then click Properties.

   The Transform Data Task Properties dialog box appears with the Source tab selected.

4. In the Description text box, type **Load ShipperList Table** and then click the Destination tab.

5. Click the Create button.

   The Create Destination Table dialog box appears, displaying the CREATE TABLE statement constructed by SQL Server.

6. In the SQL Statement text box, change the table name from Shippers to **ShipperList**.

7. Change the ShipperID from varchar (255) to **char (2)** and then click OK.

   The new table format appears in the Destination tab.

8. Click the Transformations tab.

   Notice that the default column mappings are correct.

9. Click the Options tab.

10. In the Name text box, type **C:\Labfiles\Lab 7\Ex2.txt**.

Note If your \Labfiles folder isn't stored on drive C, replace C:\ with the correct drive letter.

   Notice the additional settings on this tab, but do not change any. With large batch files, additional settings would be enabled.

11. Click OK.

12. Right-click the black transformation arrow between the Shippers Text File icon and the Connection 2 icon, and then click Execute Step.

   An Execute Step DTSStep_DTSDataPumpTask_1 message box appears, informing you that the step has executed successfully.

13. Click OK.

14. On the toolbar, click the Execute button to execute the entire package.

   An Executing DTS Package: Products List dialog box appears, displaying the progress of the package execution. When the execution has completed, a Package Execution Results message box appears, informing you that the execution of the package has completed successfully.

15. Click OK.

   Review the Executing DTS Package: ProductsList dialog box. Notice that each of the four steps completed successfully.

16. Click the Done button.

   Which steps in the DTS package are executing in parallel and which steps in the DTS package are operating in sequence?

   _____

   _____

17. On the Package menu, click Save As.

   The Save DTS Package dialog box appears.

18. In the Package Name text box, type **Reports** and then click OK.

▶ **To add data source connections**

1. From the Connection tool palette, drag the Microsoft OLE DB Provider For SQL Server icon to an open area of the workspace.

   The Connection Properties dialog box appears.

2. Click the Existing Connection option button, and verify that Connection 1 appears in the Existing Connection drop-down list.

3. Click OK.

Notice that a second Connection 1 icon appears.

4. From the Connection tool palette, drag the Microsoft OLE DB Provider For SQL Server icon to an open area of the workspace.

The Connection Properties dialog box appears.

5. Click the Existing Connection option button, and in the Existing Connection drop-down list, click Connection 2.

These new connections will be used for an ActiveX transformation task.

6. Click OK.

Notice that a second Connection 2 icon appears.

▶ **To add a data transformation task to import the employees table**

1. Verify that the new Connection 1 icon is selected, and then press Ctrl on your keyboard and click the new Connection 2 icon.

Notice that both icons are now selected.

2. Right-click either highlighted icon, and then click Transform Data Task.

A black data transformation arrow appears between the two icons, pointing to the new Connection 2 icon.

3. Right-click the new data transformation arrow, and then click Properties.

The Transform Data Task Properties dialog box appears with the Source tab selected.

4. In the Description text box, type **Load EmployeeList Table**.

5. Click the SQL Query option button.

6. In the SQL-Query text box, type the following Transact-SQL script:

```
SELECT EmployeeID, LastName, FirstName, HomePhone from Employees
```

7. Click the Preview button.

The View Data dialog box appears. Notice the list of employees. Specifically notice that the first and last names are in separate columns.

8. Click OK to close the View Data dialog box.

9. Click the Destination tab.

10. Click the Create button.

The Create Destination Table dialog box appears displaying the CREATE TABLE statement constructed by SQL Server.

11. Change the table name from New Table to **EmployeeList**.

12. Change the name of the LastName column to **FullName**.

13. Change the size of the FullName nvarchar column to **31**.

14. Delete the entire line defining the FirstName column.

15. Click OK to close the Create Destination Table dialog box.

▶ **To use ActiveX to define the data transformation**

1. Click the Transformations tab.

   Notice the predefined transformations.

2. Right-click the column mapping arrow between Last Name in the Source column and Full Name in the Destination column, and then click the Delete button.

3. In the Source column, press Ctrl on your keyboard and click FirstName.

   LastName and FirstName are selected in the Source column, and FullName is selected in the Destination column.

4. Click the New button.

   The Create New Transformation dialog box appears.

5. Click ActiveX Script, and then click OK.

   The Transformation Options dialog box appears.

6. In the Name text box, type **Concatenate Names**.

7. Click the Properties button.

   The ActiveX Script Transformation Properties dialog box appears.

8. In the script window, change the script to read as follows:

```
Function Main()
DTSDestination("FullName")=DTSSource("FirstName")+" "+DTSSource("LastName")
Main=DTSTransformStat_OK
End Function
```

9. Click the Parse button to verify the syntax of your ActiveX script.

   A DTS Designer message box appears informing you that the ActiveX script has parsed successfully.

10. Click OK.

11. Click the Test button.

12. A Testing Transformation dialog box appears displaying the progress of the package execution. When the execution completes, a Package Execution Results message box appears informing you that the package has executed successfully.

13. Click OK.

    If your test failed, make sure that you added both the first and last name columns before you started defining the transformation.

14. Click the View Results button in the Testing Transformation dialog box.

    The View Data dialog box appears.

    The concatenated names appear in the FullName list box.

15. Click OK to close the View Data dialog box.

16. Click the Done button to close the Testing Transformation dialog box.

17. Click OK to close the ActiveX Script Transformation Properties dialog box.

18. Click OK to close the Transformation Options dialog box.

    Notice the mapping arrow between LastName and FirstName in the Source column and FullName in the Destination column.

19. Click OK.

20. On the toolbar, click the Execute button.

21. An Executing DTS Package: Reports dialog box appears displaying the progress of the package execution. When the execution completes, a Package Execution Results message box appears informing you that the package execution has completed successfully.

22. Click OK.

    Notice that five separate steps executed. Three steps executed as a group, one after the other based on the completion of step 1 and the success of step 2. The other two steps executed independently of any other steps.

Note Although this package can be rerun, it is not a complete package. At a minimum, steps to delete duplicate data if the package is run multiple times are missing.

---

23. Click the Done button to close the Executing DTS Package: Reports dialog box.

24. On the toolbar, click the Save button.

25. Close the DTS Designer window by clicking its associated Close button.

▶ **To view previous versions of a DTS package**

1. In the SQL Server Enterprise Manager details pane for the Meta Data Services container, right-click Reports and then click Versions.

   The DTS Package Versions dialog box appears.

2. Click the DTS package with the earliest creation date, and then click the Edit button.

   The first version of this DTS package that you saved appears in a DTS Designer window.

3. Close the DTS Designer window.

▶ **To view meta data about a DTS package**

1. In the console tree, click Meta Data.

2. In the details pane, click the Package tab.

   The two packages you have saved to Meta Data Services appear.

3. Expand Reports, and then click the most recent package.

   Meta data about the DTS package appears. Notice that information about the author of the package, creation date, modification date and package ID is available.

Exercise 3
Importing Data Using Bcp and the BULK INSERT Statement

In this exercise, you will import data from a text file using the Bcp command prompt utility and the BULK INSERT Transact-SQL statement.

▶ **To import data using Bcp**

1. On the SQL Server Enterprise Manager Tools menu, click SQL Query Analyzer.

   SQL Query Analyzer appears. A connection is automatically established to the default instance using your Student*xx* user account.

2. On the toolbar, click the Load SQL Script button or press Ctrl+Shift+P.

   The Open Query File dialog box appears.

3. Browse to the C:\Labfiles\Lab 7 folder, and open the NewTbl.sql script.

Note If your \Labfiles folder isn't stored on drive C, replace C:\ with the correct drive letter.

---

4. Review this script, which is shown below.

```
USE ReportsDB
IF EXISTS (SELECT * FROM sysobjects WHERE name = 'newprod')
DROP TABLE ReportsDB.dbo.NewProd
CREATE TABLE dbo.NewProd
  (
  ProductID int NOT NULL ,
  ProductName nvarchar (40) NOT NULL ,
  SupplierID int NULL ,
  CategoryID int NULL ,
  QuantityPerUnit nvarchar (20) NULL ,
  UnitPrice money NULL ,
  UnitsInStock smallint NULL ,

  UnitsOnOrder smallint NULL ,

  ReorderLevel smallint NULL ,
  Discontinued bit NOT NULL   )
SELECT * FROM ReportsDB.dbo.NewProd
```

   This script will create a new table into which you will import new data.

5. Click the Execute Query button on the toolbar to execute the NewTbl.sql script.

6. Click Start, point to Programs, point to Accessories, and then click Command Prompt.

   A Command Prompt window appears.

7. Type **bcp** and then press Enter.

   Notice the display of available arguments.

8. Type the following command on a single line:

```
bcp ReportsDB..NewProd in "C:\Labfiles\Lab 7\NewProd.txt" -c -t"," -r\n -T
```

Note If your \Labfiles folder isn't stored on drive C, you need to replace C:\ with the correct drive letter in the above command.

---

9. Press Enter.

   Notice that 1343 rows are copied. The packet size used and elapsed clock time are also displayed.

10. Close the Command Prompt window.

11. In SQL Query Analyzer, highlight SELECT * FROM ReportsDB.dbo.NewProd and then click the Execute Query button on the toolbar.

    The results pane displays the new products imported into the NewProd table.

12. Click the Messages tab in the results pane.

    Notice that 1343 rows are displayed from the NewProd table.

13. Do not close SQL Query Analyzer or SQL Server Enterprise Manager.

▶ **To import data using the BULK INSERT Transact-SQL statement**

1. In SQL Query Analyzer, clear the highlight from the SELECT statement and then click the Execute Query button on the toolbar to reexecute the NewTbl.sql script.

   The existing table is dropped and re-created with no data.

2. On the toolbar, click the Load SQL Script button.

   The Open Query File dialog box appears.

3. Browse to the C:\Labfiles\Lab 7 folder, and open the BulkInsertl.sql script.

Note If your \Labfiles folder isn't stored on drive C, replace C:\ with the correct drive letter. Also, the path in the BulkInsertl.sql script assumes that the \Labfiles folder is installed on drive C. If your path is different, change the pathname in the script accordingly.

---

4. Review this script, which is shown below.

```
BULK INSERT ReportsDB.dbo.NewProd
FROM 'C:\Labfiles\Lab 7\NewProd.txt'
WITH
(
```

```
DATAFILETYPE = 'char' ,
FIELDTERMINATOR = ',' ,
ROWTERMINATOR = '\n'
)
SELECT * FROM ReportsDB.dbo.NewProd
```

This script will create a new table into which you will import new data. Notice that the information supplied to import the file is similar to the information supplied to import the same text file using Bcp.

5. On the toolbar, click the Execute Query button.

The results pane displays the new products imported into the NewProd table.

6. Click the Messages tab in the results pane.

Notice that 1343 rows were copied.

7. Close SQL Query Analyzer.

8. Close SQL Server Enterprise Manager.

9. Log off your computer.

Lab 6: Performing Database Backups and Restorations

Objectives

After completing this lab, you will be able to

- Create permanent backup devices
- Perform backups using the Create Backup wizard
- Perform backups directly using SQL Server Enterprise Manager
- Perform backups using Transact-SQL
- Perform a full database restoration using SQL Server Enterprise Manager
- Perform a partial database restoration using SQL Server Enterprise Manager
- Perform a database restoration using Transact-SQL
- Restore the master database

Before You Begin

You must successfully complete Exercises 1 and 2 in Lab 1 before you begin this lab.

Note You must log on to your student computer using the correct domain user account to have sufficient permissions to perform the lab exercises in this Lab Manual.

Estimated time to complete this lab: 90 minutes

Exercise 1
Creating Permanent Backup Devices

In this exercise, you use SQL Server Enterprise Manager and Transact-SQL to create permanent backup devices.

▶ **To create a permanent backup device using SQL Server Enterprise Manager**

1. Press Ctrl+Alt+Del to log on to the Contoso.msft domain.

   The Log On To Windows screen appears.

2. Verify that the User Name text box displays Student*xx* (where *xx* is your computer number).

3. Verify that the Log On To text box displays Contoso. (If the Log On To text box does not appear, click the Options button.)

4. In the Password text box, type **password** and then click OK.

   Personal settings are applied, and you are logged on to Microsoft Windows 2000.

5. Click Start, point to Programs, point to Microsoft SQL Server, and then click Enterprise Manager.

   SQL Server Enterprise Manager appears displaying the Microsoft SQL Servers and the Event Viewer (Local) console trees in the console root.

6. In the console tree, expand the Microsoft SQL Servers container, expand the SQL Server Group container, expand the Server*xx* container (the default container), and then expand the Management container.

7. In the console tree, right-click the Backup container and then click New Backup Device.

   A Backup Device Properties – New Device dialog box appears.

8. In the Name text box, type **MasterBackupDevice** and then click OK.

   MasterBackupDevice is created in the Backup folder (\Program Files\Microsoft SQL Server\Backup) on the C drive and appears in the details pane for the Backup container.

▶ **To create a permanent backup device using Transact-SQL**

1. On the Tools menu, click SQL Query Analyzer, and then expand the SQL Query Analyzer window.

   You are connected to SQL Query Analyzer as Contoso\Student*xx*.

2. On the toolbar, click the Load SQL Script button.

   The Open Query File dialog box appears.

3. Open BackupDevices.sql in the C:\Labfiles\Lab 9 folder.

Note If your \Labfiles folder isn't stored on drive C, replace C:\ with the correct drive letter. Also, the path in the BackupDevices.sql script presumes that SQL Server 2000 is installed on drive C, and that, in step 9, you will create the C:\SQLBackups folder on drive C. If your path is different, change the pathname in the script accordingly.

A Transact-SQL script appears that will create four permanent backup devices using the following logical names: MSDBBackup, NWCopyFullBackup, NWCopyDiffBackup, and NWCopyTLogBackup. The specified physical path does not yet exist. You will create this folder in just a few moments.

4. Click the Execute Query button to execute the BackupDevices.sql script.

Notice that the script added four disk devices. SQL Server 2000 does not verify the physical path for a backup device until you are ready to use the backup device.

5. On the toolbar, click the Clear Window button.

6. In the query pane, type **sp_helpdevice** and then click the Execute Query button on the toolbar.

Notice that five disk devices appear, along with information regarding the master, model, and tempdb database files.

7. Minimize SQL Query Analyzer.

8. Open Windows Explorer by clicking Start, pointing to Programs, pointing to Accessories, and then clicking Windows Explorer.

9. Create a folder on the C drive called SQLBackups.

Note The path in step 9 presumes that SQL Server 2000 is installed on drive C. If SQL Server 2000 isn't installed on drive C, substitute C:\ with the correct drive letter.

10. Close Windows Explorer.

11. Switch to SQL Server Enterprise Manager.

12. In the console tree, in the Management container, right-click the Backup container, and then click Refresh.

13. Click the Backup container.

The details pane displays all five permanent backup devices.

Exercise 2
Performing Backups Using SQL Server Enterprise Manager

In this exercise, you will back up the master database using the Create Backup wizard.

▶ **To back up the master database using the Create Backup wizard**

1. Verify that you are switched to SQL Server Enterprise Manager.

2. In the console tree, click the default instance.

3. On the Tools menu, click Wizards.

   The Select Wizard dialog box appears.

4. Expand Management, and then double-click Backup Wizard.

   The Welcome To The Create Database Backup Wizard screen appears.

5. Click Next.

   The Select Database To Backup page appears.

6. In the Database drop-down list, select master and then click Next.

   The Type Name And Description For Backup page appears.

7. In the Name text box, type **Master Database Backup #1**.

8. In the Description text box, type **Backup Set #1** and then click Next.

   The Select Type Of Backup page appears. Notice that you can perform only a full database backup of the master database.

9. Click Next.

   The Select Backup Destination And Action page appears.

10. Click the Backup Device option button and then, in the Backup Device drop-down list, select MasterBackupDevice.

11. Click the Overwrite The Backup Media option button.

12. Select the Read And Verify The Integrity Of The Backup After Backup check box, and then click Next.

    The Initialize Media page appears.

13. Select the Initialize And Label Media check box.

14. In the Media Set Name text box, type **MasterBackups**.

15. In the Media Set Description text box, type **Media for Master Database Backups** and then click Next.

    The Backup Verification And Scheduling page appears.

16. Select the Backup Set Will Expire check box, and then click Next.

    The Completing The Create Database Backup Wizard page appears. Review the details of the backup you have defined.

17. Click the Finish button.

The Backup Progress dialog box appears, displaying the progress of the backup of the master database. Next, the Verify Progress dialog box appears, displaying the progress of the verification of the master database backup. When the database backup is complete, a Wizard Complete! message box appears.

18. Click OK to close the Wizard Complete! message box.

19. Do not close SQL Server Enterprise Manager.

▶ **To back up a database using SQL Server Enterprise Manager directly**

1. In the SQL Server Enterprise Manager console tree, expand the Databases container in the default instance.

2. In the console tree, right-click msdb, point to All Tasks, and then click Backup Database.

The SQL Server Backup - Msdb dialog box appears with the General tab selected.

3. In the Name text box, type **Msdb Database Backup #1**.

4. In the Description text box, type **Backup Set #1**.

5. In the Destination group box, click the Add button.

The Select Backup Destination dialog box appears.

6. Click the Backup Device option button.

7. Select MSDBBackup from the Backup Device drop-down list, and then click OK.

In the Destination group box, the MSDBBackup device appears as the backup destination.

8. Click the Overwrite Existing Media option button and then click the Options tab.

9. In the Options group box, select the Verify Backup Upon Completion check box.

10. In the Media Set Labels group box, select the Initialize And Label Media check box.

11. In the Media Set Name text box, type **MsdbBackups**.

12. In the Media Set Description text box, type **Media for msdb Database Backups** and then click OK.

The Backup Progress dialog box appears displaying the progress of the backup of the msdb database. Next, the Verify Progress dialog box appears displaying the progress of the verification of the msdb database backup. When the database backup is complete, a SQL Server Enterprise Manager message box appears.

13. Click OK to close the SQL Server Enterprise Manager message box.

14. Do not close SQL Server Enterprise Manager.

Exercise 3
Performing Backups Using Transact-SQL

In this exercise, you attach the NWCopy database to the default SQL Server instance. You will then perform a full database backup. You modify data in the database and perform a transaction log backup. You perform an additional modification to the same data and a differential database backup. You perform an additional modification to the database and a transaction log backup. You perform one more modification and another transaction log backup.

▶ **To attach the NWCopy database to use for this lab**

1. Switch to SQL Query Analyzer.

2. On the toolbar, click the Load SQL Script button.

   A SQL Query Analyzer dialog box appears asking whether you want to save any changes.

3. Click the No button.

   The Open Query File dialog box appears.

4. Open NWCopy.sql in the C:\Labfiles\Lab 9 folder.

Note If your \Labfiles folder isn't stored on drive C, replace C:\ with the correct drive letter. You will also need to change the path in the NWCopy.sql script.

A Transact-SQL script appears that will attach the NWCopy database for use in the remainder of this lab.

5. Click the Execute Query button to execute the NWCopy.sql script.

   Notice that the command completes successfully.

▶ **To perform a full database backup using Transact-SQL**

1. On the SQL Query Analyzer toolbar, click the Load SQL Script button.

   The Open Query File dialog box appears.

2. Open NWCopyFullBackup.sql in the C:\Labfiles\Lab 9 folder.

Note If your \Labfiles folder isn't stored on drive C, replace C:\ with the correct drive letter.

A Transact-SQL script appears that will perform a full database backup of the NWCopy database.

3. Click the Execute Query button to execute the NWCopyFullBackup.sql script.

   In the results pane, notice that the NWCopy database is backed up, including one page from the transaction log. Also notice performance statistics for this backup.

▶ **To modify data and perform a transaction log backup using Transact-SQL**

1. On the SQL Query Analyzer toolbar, click the Load SQL Script button.

   The Open Query File dialog box appears.

2. Open NWCopy_TLog1.sql in the C:\Labfiles\Lab 9 folder.

Note If your \Labfiles folder isn't stored on drive C, replace C:\ with the correct drive letter.

A Transact-SQL script appears that will modify data to the NWCopy database and then perform a transaction log backup of the NWCopy database.

3. Click the Execute Query button to execute the NWCopy_TLog1.sql script.

   In the results pane of the Messages tab, notice that the NWCopy transaction log is backed up. Also, notice performance statistics for this backup. Finally in the results pane of the Grids tab, notice the changed contact name.

▶ **To modify data and perform a differential database backup using Transact-SQL**

1. On the SQL Query Analyzer toolbar, click the Load SQL Script button.

   The Open Query File dialog box appears.

2. Open NWCopy_Diff.sql in the C:\Labfiles\Lab 9 folder.

Note If your \Labfiles folder isn't stored on drive C, replace C:\ with the correct drive letter.

A Transact-SQL script appears that will modify data to the NWCopy database and then perform a differential database backup of the NWCopy database.

3. Click the Execute Query button to execute the NWCopy_Diff.sql script.

   In the results pane of the Messages tab, notice that the NWCopy database is backed up, including one page from the transaction log. Also notice performance statistics for this backup. Finally in the results pane of the Grids tab, notice the changed contact name.

▶ **To modify data and perform a transaction log database backup using Transact-SQL**

1. On the SQL Query Analyzer toolbar, click the Load SQL Script button.

   The Open Query File dialog box appears.

2. Open NWCopy_TLog2.sql in the C:\Labfiles\Lab 9 folder.

Note If your \Labfiles folder isn't stored on drive C, replace C:\ with the correct drive letter.

A Transact-SQL script appears that will modify data to the NWCopy database and then perform a transaction log backup of the NWCopy database.

3. Click the Execute Query button to execute the NWCopy_TLog2.sql script.

In the results pane of the Messages tab, notice that the NWCopy transaction log is backed up. Also notice performance statistics for this backup. Finally in the results pane of the Grids tab, notice the changed contact name.

▶   **To modify data and perform a transaction log database backup using Transact-SQL**

1. On the SQL Query Analyzer toolbar, click the Load SQL Script button.

The Open Query File dialog box appears.

2. Open NWCopy_TLog3.sql in the C:\Labfiles\Lab 9 folder.

Note If your \Labfiles folder isn't stored on drive C, replace C:\ with the correct drive letter.

A Transact-SQL script appears that will modify data to the NWCopy database and then perform a transaction log backup of the NWCopy database.

3. Click the Execute Query button to execute the NWCopy_TLog3.sql script.

In the results pane of the Messages tab, notice that the NWCopy transaction log is backed up. Also notice the performance statistics for this backup. Finally in the results pane of the Grids tab, notice the changed contact name.

Exercise 4
Retrieving Backup Media Information

In this exercise, you will retrieve backup media information from a backup device using SQL Server Enterprise Manager and Transact-SQL.

▶ **To retrieve backup media information using Transact-SQL**

1. On the SQL Query Analyzer toolbar, click the Load SQL Script button.

   The Open Query File dialog box appears.

2. Open QueryHeaders.sql in the C:\Labfiles\Lab 9 folder.

Note If your \Labfiles folder isn't stored on drive C, replace C:\ with the correct drive letter.

A Transact-SQL script appears, containing five separate queries, which will retrieve information from the NWCopyTLogBackup backup device.

3. On the toolbar, click the Execute Query button to execute the QueryHeaders.sql script.

   In the results pane, notice five separate result sets. The first result set displays information regarding the media set itself. The second result set displays information regarding each backup set recorded on this backup media. The final three result sets display information regarding each data and transaction log file in each of the three backup sets recorded on this backup media.

▶ **To retrieve backup media information using SQL Server Enterprise Manager**

1. Switch to SQL Server Enterprise Manager.

2. In the console tree of the default instance in the Management container, click the Backup container.

   The backup devices for this SQL Server 2000 instance are displayed in the details pane.

3. In the details pane, right-click NWCopyTLogBackup and then click Properties.

   The Backup Device Properties – NWCopyTLogBackup dialog box appears displaying the filename associated with this backup device.

4. Click the View Contents button.

   The View Backup Media Contents dialog box appears, displaying the contents of the NWCopyTLogBackup device. Details regarding three transaction log backup sets appear.

5. Compare the backup set information displayed when using the View Backup Media Contents dialog box in SQL Server Enterprise Manager and when using the Transact-SQL queries in the previous procedure.

6. Click the Close button to close the View Backup Media Contents dialog box, and then click Cancel to close the Backup Device Properties – NWCopyTLogBackup dialog box.

7. Close SQL Query Analyzer.

8. Do not close SQL Server Enterprise Manager.

Exercise 5
Performing a Full Database Restoration Using SQL Server Enterprise Manager

In this exercise, you will use SQL Server Enterprise Manager to perform a full database restoration and recovery.

▶ **To damage the NWCopy database**

1. In the SQL Server Enterprise Manager console tree, right-click your default instance and then click Stop.

   A SQL Server Enterprise Manager dialog box appears asking whether you are sure you want to stop the SQL Server Service.

2. Click the Yes button.

   A Service Control Failure dialog box appears informing you that SQLServerAgent is dependent on the SQL Server Service and asking whether you want to stop it also.

3. Click the Yes button.

4. Click the Start button, and then click Run.

   The Run dialog box appears.

5. In the Open drop-down combo box, type **C:\Labfiles\Lab 9** and then click OK.

Note If your \Labfiles folder isn't stored on drive C, replace C:\ with the correct drive letter.

---

6. Delete the NWCopy.mdf file.

   A Confirm File Delete dialog box appears asking whether you are sure you want to delete this file.

7. Click the Yes button.

8. Close Windows Explorer.

▶ **To back up the active portion of the NWCopy transaction log**

1. In the SQL Server Enterprise Manager console tree, expand your default instance.

   After a few moments, notice that SQL Server Enterprise Manager starts the SQL Server service and connects to the default instance.

2. In the console tree, click the Databases container.

   The databases appear in the details pane, with the NWCopy database marked as suspect (because you deleted the data file).

3. In the details pane, right-click NWCopy (Suspect), point to All Tasks, and then click Backup Database.

   The SQL Server Backup – NWCopy dialog box appears.

4. Click the Transaction Log option button.

5. In the Destination group box, click the Add button.

   The Select Backup Destination dialog box appears.

6. Click the Backup Device option button, and then select NWCopyTLogBackup in the Backup Device drop-down list.

7. Click OK.

   NWCOPYTLogBackup appears as the only device listed in the Destination group box.

8. Verify that the Append To Media option button is selected.

9. Click the Options tab.

10. Clear the Remove Inactive Entries From Transaction Log check box so that none of the entries are truncated.

11. In the Media Set Name text box, type **NWCopyTLogBackup**.

    Why are the options in the Media Set Labels group box grayed?

    _____

    _____

12. Click OK.

    The Backup Progress dialog box appears displaying the progress of the backup. When the backup has completed, a SQL Server Enterprise Manager message box appears stating the backup operation was a success.

13. Click OK.

    Why is it necessary to back up the active portion of the NWCopy transaction log?

    _____

    _____

    Why is the Without Truncation option required?

    _____

    _____

▶ **To perform a complete restoration using SQL Server Enterprise Manager**

1. In the SQL Server Enterprise Manager console tree, right-click NWCopy, point to All Tasks, and then click Restore Database.

The Restore Database dialog box appears, displaying the backup sets required to completely restore the NWCopy database. Notice SQL Server Enterprise Manager has selected the original full database backup, the differential database backup, and all transaction log backups since the differential database backup. (A total of three out of four transaction logs are selected.)

2. Click OK to completely restore the NWCopy database.

A series of Restore Progress dialog boxes appear displaying the progress of the restoration. When the restoration is complete, a SQL Server Enterprise Manager message box appears stating that the restoration of the NWCopy database was completed successfully.

3. Click OK.

4. In the console tree, expand NWCopy and then click Tables.

The tables in the NWCopy database appear in the details pane.

5. In the details pane, right-click Customers, point to Open Table, and then click Return Top.

The Number Of Rows dialog box appears.

6. In the Maximum Number Of Rows To Fetch text box, type **1** and then click OK.

A Data In Table 'Customers' In 'NWCopy' On 'Server*xx*' window appears displaying the top row of the Customers table after the restoration. Verify that the Contact Name is 4_Maria Anders. This was the most recent change made to the database.

7. Close the Data In Table 'Customers' In 'NWCopy' On 'Server*xx*' window.

8. Do not close SQL Server Enterprise Manager.

Exercise 6
Performing a Partial Database Restoration Using SQL Server Enterprise Manager

In this exercise, you will restore the full database backup of the NWCopy database to standby mode and then view the restored data. Next, you will restore the first transaction log backup to standby mode and then view the restored data. Then you will restore and recover the second transaction log backup to a specified point in time.

▶ **To restore a full database backup to standby mode**

1. In the SQL Server Enterprise Manager console tree, right-click NWCopy, point to All Tasks, and then click Restore Database.

   The Restore Database dialog box appears, displaying the backup sets required to completely restore the NWCopy database. Notice SQL Server Enterprise Manager has selected the original full database backup, the differential database backup, and all transaction log backups since the differential database backup. (A total of three out of four transaction logs are selected.)

2. In the Parameters group box, clear all backup sets selected by SQL Server Enterprise Manager other than the Full NWCopy Database Backup #1 backup set check box. Verify that no other backup sets are selected.

3. Click the Options tab.

4. Click the Leave Database Read-Only And Able To Restore Additional Transaction Logs option button, and then click OK.

   A Restore Progress dialog box appears displaying the progress of the restoration. When the restoration is complete, a SQL Server Enterprise Manager message box appears stating that the restoration of the NWCopy database was completed successfully.

5. Click OK.

   In the console tree, notice the NWCopy database indicates that it is Read-Only.

6. In the console tree, click the Tables container in the NWCopy container.

   The tables in the NWCopy database appear in the details pane.

7. In the details pane, right-click Customers, point to Open Table, and then click Return Top.

   The Number Of Rows dialog box appears.

8. In the Maximum Number Of Rows To Fetch text box, type **1** and then click OK.

   The Data In Table 'Customers' In 'NWCopy' On 'Server*xx*' window appears displaying the top row of the Customers table after the restoration. Verify that the Contact Name is Maria Anders.

9. Close the Data In Table 'Customers' In 'NWCopy' On 'Server*xx*' window.

▶   **To continue restoring a database using a transaction log backup**

1. In the SQL Server Enterprise Manager console tree, right-click NWCopy, point to All Tasks, and then click Restore Database.

   The Restore Database dialog box appears, displaying the backup sets required to completely restore the NWCopy database. Notice that SQL Server Enterprise Manager has selected all the transaction log backups.

   Why wasn't the differential database backup selected?

   _____

   _____

2. In the Parameters group box, clear all backup sets selected by SQL Server Enterprise Manager and then select the first NWCopy Transaction Log backup (NWCopy Transaction Log Backup #1). Verify that no other backup sets are selected.

3. Click the Options tab.

4. Click the Leave Database Read-Only And Able To Restore Additional Transaction Logs option button, and then click OK.

   The Restore Progress dialog box appears displaying the progress of the restoration. When the restoration is complete, a SQL Server Enterprise Manager message box appears stating that the restoration of the NWCopy database was completed successfully.

5. Click OK.

   In the console tree, notice the NWCopy database indicates that it is Read-Only.

6. In the console tree, click the Tables container in the NWCopy container.

   The tables in the NWCopy database appear in the details pane.

7. In the details pane, right-click Customers, point to Open Table, and then click Return Top.

   The Number Of Rows dialog box appears.

8. In the text box, type **1** and then click OK.

   The Data In Table 'Customers' In 'NWCopy' On 'Server*xx*' window appears displaying the top row of the Customers table after the restoration. Verify that the Contact Name is 1_Maria Anders.

9. Close the Data In Table 'Customers' In 'NWCopy' On 'Server*xx*' window.

▶   **To restore and recover to a point in time**

1. In the SQL Server Enterprise Manager console tree, right-click NWCopy, point to All Tasks, and then click Restore Database.

   The Restore Database dialog box appears, displaying the backup sets required to completely restore the NWCopy database. Notice SQL Server Enterprise Manager has selected the three remaining transaction log backups.

2. In the Parameters group box, clear all backup sets selected by SQL Server Enterprise Manager and then select the second NWCopy Transaction Log backup (NWCopy Transaction Log Backup #2). Verify that no other backup sets are selected.

3. Select the Point In Time Restore check box.

   The Point In Time Restore dialog box appears.

4. Click OK to use the time provided.

   In a larger transaction log, you would select a time within the transaction log. However, in this lab scenario, only one transaction occurs in each transaction log backup.

5. Click OK to perform the point-in-time restoration.

   The Restore Progress dialog box appears displaying the progress of the restoration. When the process is finished, a SQL Server Enterprise Manager message box appears stating that the restoration of the NWCopy database was completed successfully.

6. Click OK.

   Can additional transaction logs be applied to the NWCopy database?

   _____

   _____

7. In the console tree, click the Tables container in the NWCopy container.

   The tables in the NWCopy database appear in the details pane.

8. In the details pane, right-click Customers, point to Open Table, and then click Return Top.

   The Number Of Rows dialog box appears.

9. In the text box, type **1** and then click OK.

   The Data In Table 'Customers' In 'NWCopy' On 'Serverxx' window appears displaying the top row of the Customers table after the restoration. Verify that the Contact Name is 2_Maria Anders.

10. Close the Data In Table 'Customers' In 'NWCopy' On 'Serverxx' window.

11. Close SQL Server Enterprise Manager.

Exercise 7
Restoring the Master Database

In this exercise, you will start SQL Server in single-user mode and restore the master database from backup.

▶ **To start SQL Server in single-user mode**

1. On the Windows taskbar, right-click SQL Server Service Manager and then click MSSQLServer – Stop.

   A SQL Server Service Manager dialog box appears asking whether you want to stop the MSSQLServer on \\Server*xx*.

2. Click the Yes button.

3. Click the Start button, and then click Run.

   The Run dialog box appears.

4. In the Open drop-down combo box, type **sqlservr -m** and then click OK.

   A command prompt window appears, and SQL Server starts in single-user mode. Notice that the command prompt windows remains open.

▶ **To restore the master database**

1. Click the Start button, point to Programs, point to Microsoft SQL Server, and then click Query Analyzer.

   The Connect To SQL Server dialog box appears.

2. Verify that the Windows Authentication option button is selected, and then click OK.

3. In the query pane, type **RESTORE DATABASE MASTER FROM MasterBackupDevice**.

4. On the toolbar, click the Execute Query button.

   Notice that the master database is successfully restored. Also notice that SQL Server is shut down and the command prompt window is closed.

5. Close SQL Query Analyzer. Do not save any changes.

6. Click the Start button, point to Programs, point to Microsoft SQL Server, and then click Enterprise Manager.

7. Expand Microsoft SQL Servers, expand the SQL Server group, and then expand the default instance.

   After a few moments, SQL Server starts.

8. Expand the Databases container.

   Does the NWCopy database appear in the list of databases? Why or why not?

What is the simplest way to restore the NWCopy database?

_____

_____

9. Close SQL Server Enterprise Manager.

10. Log off your computer.

Lab 7: Managing Access to Microsoft SQL Server 2000

Objectives

After completing this lab, you will be able to

- Change SQL Server authentication modes
- Create and manage logins using SQL Server Enterprise Manager
- Create and manage logins using Transact-SQL and SQL Server Enterprise Manager
- View SQL Server access information using SQL Server Enterprise Manager and Transact-SQL

Before You Begin

You must successfully complete Exercises 1 and 2 in Lab 1 before you begin this lab.

Note You must log on to your student computer using the correct domain user account to have sufficient permissions to perform the lab exercises in this Lab Manual.

Estimated time to complete this lab: 75 minutes

Exercise 1
Configuring Windows Authentication Mode

In this exercise, you will use SQL Query Analyzer and attempt to connect to SQL Server using the sa system administrator account. Next, you will change the SQL Server authentication mode. Finally, you will use SQL Query Analyzer to connect to SQL Server using the sa system administrator account.

▶ **To attempt to connect to SQL Server using the sa system administrator account**

1. Press Ctrl+Alt+Del to log on to the Contoso.msft domain.

   The Log On To Windows screen appears.

2. Verify that the User Name text box displays Student*xx* (where *xx* is your computer number).

3. Verify that the Log On To text box displays Contoso. (If the Log On To text box does not appear, click the Options button.)

4. In the Password text box, type **password** and then click OK.

   Personal settings are applied, and you are logged on to Microsoft Windows 2000.

5. Click Start, point to Programs, point to Microsoft SQL Server, and then click Query Analyzer.

   The Connect To SQL Server dialog box appears.

6. Verify that the Windows Authentication option button is selected, and then click OK to connect to the default instance.

   You connect to SQL Server using a trusted connection.

7. In the query pane, type **EXEC xp_loginconfig 'login mode'** and then click the Execute Query button on the toolbar.

   The results pane displays the configured login mode.

   In what authentication mode is SQL Server running?

   _____

8. On the File menu, click Connect.

   The Connect To SQL Server dialog box appears.

9. In the Connect Using group box, click the SQL Server Authentication option button.

10. In the Login Name text box, type **sa** and then click OK.

    A SQL Query Analyzer message box appears stating that the login failed for user 'sa' because it was not associated with a trusted SQL Server connection.

11. Click OK to close the SQL Query Analyzer message box.

12. Do not close SQL Query Analyzer or the Connect To SQL Server dialog box.

▶ **To change the SQL Server Authentication Mode and then test the change**

1. Click Start, point to Programs, point to Microsoft SQL Server, and then click Enterprise Manager.

   SQL Server Enterprise Manager appears displaying the Microsoft SQL Servers and the Event Viewer (Local) console trees in the console root.

2. In the console tree, expand the Microsoft SQL Servers container and then expand the SQL Server Group container.

3. Right-click the Server*xx* container (the default instance), and then click Properties.

   The SQL Server Properties (Configure) – Server*xx* dialog box appears with the General tab selected.

4. Click the Security tab.

   Notice that the Windows Only option button is selected to set authentication to Windows only.

5. In the Security group box, click the SQL Server And Windows option button and then click OK.

   A SQL Server Enterprise Manager – Server*xx* dialog box appears asking whether you wish to stop and restart the SQL Server service now.

6. Click the Yes button.

   The SQL Server service is restarted using Mixed Mode authentication.

7. Switch to SQL Query Analyzer.

8. In the Connect To SQL Server dialog box, click OK to connect to SQL Server using the sa login account with no password.

   You are connected to SQL Server using the sa login account.

9. In the query pane, type **EXEC xp_loginconfig 'login mode'** and then click the Execute Query button on the toolbar.

   The results pane displays the configured login mode.

   In what authentication mode is SQL Server running?

---

10. Do not close SQL Query Analyzer or SQL Server Enterprise Manager.

Exercise 2
Creating and Managing Logins Using SQL Server Enterprise Manager

In this exercise, you will use the Create Login wizard to create a SQL Server login account and then grant the login access to SQL Server and the NWCopy database. You will use the Create Login wizard to create a login for a Windows user account and then deny that user access to SQL Server. You will then use SQL Server Enterprise Manager to create a login for an existing Windows group and also create a second SQL Server login account. Next, you will modify the sa login account by creating a password for the account. Finally, you will remove the local Administrators group login from the Logins container.

▶ **To attach the NWCopy database to use for this lab**

1. On the SQL Query Analyzer toolbar, click the Load SQL Script button.

   A SQL Query Analyzer dialog box appears asking whether you want to save any changes.

2. Click the No button.

   The Open Query File dialog box appears.

3. Open NWCopy.sql in the C:\Labfiles\Lab 10 folder.

Note If your \Labfiles folder isn't stored on drive C, replace C:\ with the correct drive letter. You also need to change the path in the NWCopy.sql script.

A Transact-SQL script appears that will attach the NWCopy database for use in the remainder of this lab.

4. On the toolbar, click the Execute Query button to execute the NWCopy.sql script.

   Notice that the command completes successfully.

5. Switch to SQL Server Enterprise Manager.

6. In the console tree, expand the default instance and then click the Databases container.

7. On the toolbar, click the Refresh button.

▶ **To create a SQL Server login using the Create Login wizard**

1. In SQL Server Enterprise Manager console tree, click the default instance.

2. On the View menu, click Taskpad.

   The taskpad for the default instance appears in the details pane.

3. In the details pane, click the Wizards tab.

   The SQL Server wizards appear in the details pane taskpad.

4. Under Setup A Database, click Create A Login.

   The Welcome To The Create Login wizard screen appears.

5. Click Next.

   The Select Authentication Mode For This Login page appears.

6. Click the SQL Server Login Information That Was Assigned To Me By The System Administrator (SQL Server Authentication) option button, and then click Next.

   The Authentication With SQL Server page appears.

7. In the Login ID text box, type **Smoky**.

8. In the Password text box and the Confirm Password text box, type **password** and then click Next.

   The Grant Access To Security Roles page appears.

9. In the Server Roles list box, select the Security Administrators check box and then click Next.

   The Grant Access To Databases page appears.

10. In the Permit In Database list box, select the NWCopy check box to permit access to this database only and then click Next.

    The Completing The Create Login Wizard page appears. Review the details of the login you have defined.

11. Click the Finish button.

    After the login is successfully created, a Wizard Complete! message box appears.

12. Click OK to close the Wizard Complete! message box.

13. In the console tree, expand the default instance, expand the Security container, and then click the Logins container.

    In the details pane, notice that Smoky appears as a standard type of login.

▶ **To create a login for a Windows user using the Create Login wizard**

1. In the SQL Server Enterprise Manager console tree, click the default instance.

2. In the details pane, click the Wizards tab.

   The SQL Server wizards appear in the details pane.

3. Under Setup A Database, click Create A Login.

   The Welcome To The Create Login Wizard screen appears.

4. Click Next.

   The Select Authentication Mode For This Login page appears.

5. Click the Windows Account Information I Use To Logon To My Computer (Windows Authentication) option button, and then click Next.

   The Authentication With Windows page appears.

6. In the Windows Account text box, type **Contoso\TestUser*xx*** (where *xx* is your computer number).

7. In the Security Access group box, click the Deny Access To The Server option button and then click Next.

   The Completing The Create Login Wizard page appears. Review the details of the login you have defined.

8. Click the Finish button.

   After the login is created, a Wizard Complete! message box appears.

9. Click OK to close the Wizard Complete! message box.

10. In the console tree, click the Logins container.

    In the details pane, notice that Contoso\TestUser*xx* appears as a Windows User type of login.

▶ **To test the new SQL Server login**

1. Switch to SQL Query Analyzer.

2. On the File menu, click Connect.

   The Connect To SQL Server dialog box appears.

3. Select the SQL Server Authentication option button.

4. In the Login Name text box, type **Smoky**.

5. In the Password text box, type **password** and then click OK.

   You are connected to the default instance of SQL Server 2000 using the SQL Server login Smoky. Notice that the title bar indicates you are connecting as Smoky.

6. On the toolbar, select NWCopy from the database drop-down list.

   Notice that the databases list contains only those databases to which Smoky has access, including system databases. All other databases are hidden.

7. In the query pane, type **SELECT * FROM Customers**.

8. On the toolbar, click the Execute Query button.

   Notice that although Smoky has access to the NWCopy database, Smoky does not have SELECT permission on the Customers object. Chapter 11 will cover permissions in more detail.

9. Close SQL Query Analyzer. Do not save any changes.

10. Do not close SQL Server Enterprise Manager.

▶ **To create a login for a Windows group using SQL Server Enterprise Manager directly**

1. Switch to SQL Server Enterprise Manager.

2. In the console tree, click the Security container in the default instance.

3. In the console tree, right-click Logins, and then click New Login.

A SQL Server Login Properties – New Login dialog box appears with the General tab selected.

4. In the Name text box, type **SQL Users**.

5. In the Domain drop-down list, click Contoso.

   Notice that the name SQL Users in the Name text box now reads Contoso\SQL Users.

Note The Contoso\SQL Users group contains the following Windows accounts: Student01 – Student12, TestUser01 – TestUser12, and AccountingUser01 – AccountingUser12.

---

6. Click the Database Access tab.

7. Select the NWCopy check box in the Permit column.

   Notice that the public role is selected by default. You cannot drop a login from the public role.

8. Click OK to create this new login.

   The new login appears in the details pane for the Logins container.

   What is the effective permission of the TestUser*xx* account? Explain.

   _____

   Do you have permission to log in to the default instance of SQL Server on your partner's computer? Explain.

   _____

9. Do not close SQL Server Enterprise Manager.

▶ **To review and modify the sa login account**

1. In the details pane for the Logins container, right-click sa and then click Properties.

   The SQL Server Login Properties – Sa dialog box appears with the General tab selected.

2. In the Password text box, type **pass**.

3. Click the Server Roles tab.

   Notice the sa login account is a member of the System Administrators server role. This cannot be changed.

4. Click the Database Access tab.

   Notice the sa login account is a member of the db_owner database role in every database.

5. Click OK.

   A Confirm Password dialog box appears.

6. In the Confirm New Password text box, type **pass** and then click OK.

▶ **To delete the Builtin\Administrators login**

1. In the details pane for the Logins container, right-click Builtin\Administrators and then click Properties.

   The SQL Server Login Properties – Builtin\Administrators dialog box appears with the General tab selected.

2. Click the Server Roles tab.

   Notice that the Builtin\Administrators login account is a member of the System Administrators server role. This cannot be changed.

3. Click the Database Access tab.

   Notice that the Builtin\Administrators login account is a member of the db_owner database role in every database.

4. Click OK.

5. In the details pane, right-click Builtin\Administrators and then click Delete.

   A Builtin\Administrators dialog box appears asking whether you are sure you wish to remove this login.

6. Click the Yes button.

   What login accounts have permission to administer SQL Server? What level of permission does each login account have?

   _____

   _____

   _____

   _____

   Does your Student*xx* account still have permission to administer SQL Server?

   _____

▶ **To attempt to add the SQL Admins group to the System Administrators server role**

1. In the console tree of the Security container, click the Server Roles container.

   The server roles appear in the details pane.

2. In the details pane, double-click System Administrators.

   The Server Role Properties – Sysadmin dialog box appears. Notice that the Contoso\SQLService and the sa logins are members of this server role.

3. Click the Add button.

   The Add Members dialog box appears. Notice that only existing logins can be added to a server role using SQL Server Enterprise Manager.

4. Click Cancel to close the Add Members dialog box, and then click Cancel again to close the Server Role Properties – Sysadmin dialog box.

Exercise 3
Creating and Managing Logins Using Transact-SQL

In this exercise, you use a Transact-SQL script to add the SQL Admins Windows group to the System Administrator server role. You also use a Transact-SQL script to attach the Accounting database and grant the Accounting group and the Smoky login access to that database. You also use a Transact-SQL script to create a user-defined database role and add the Smoky login account to that role.

▶ **To add the SQL Admins group to the System Administrator server role**

1. On the Tools menu in SQL Server Enterprise Manager, click SQL Query Analyzer.

   You are connected to SQL Query Analyzer using your Contoso\Student*xx* account.

2. On the toolbar, click the Load SQL Script button.

   The Open Query File dialog box appears.

3. Open SQLAdmins.sql in the C:\Labfiles\Lab 10 folder.

Note If your \Labfiles folder isn't stored on drive C, replace C:\ with the correct drive letter.

   A Transact-SQL script appears that will add the SQL Admins group to the System Administrator server role.

4. On the toolbar, click the Execute Query button to execute the SQLAdmins.sql script.

   Notice that Student*xx* does not have sufficient permissions to perform this action.

5. On the File menu, click Connect.

   The Connect To SQL Server dialog box appears.

6. In the Connect Using group box, click the SQL Server Authentication option button.

7. In the Login Name box, type **sa**.

8. In the Password box, type **pass** and then click OK.

   You are connected to SQL Server using the sa login account.

9. On the toolbar, click the Load SQL Script button.

   The Open Query File dialog box appears.

10. Open SQLAdmins.sql in the C:\Labfiles\Lab 10 folder.

Note If your \Labfiles folder isn't stored on drive C, replace C:\ with the correct drive letter.

---

11. On the toolbar, click the Execute Query button to execute the SQLAdmins.sql script.

    Notice that the command completes successfully.

Note The Contoso\SQL Admins group contains the following Windows accounts: Student01 – Student12.

---

12. On the File menu, click Disconnect All.
13. Switch to SQL Server Enterprise Manager.
14. In the console tree, click the Logins container.
15. On the toolbar, click the Refresh button.

    In the details pane, notice the Contoso\SQL Admins group has a login that was granted via membership in the System Administrators server role.

    Does your Student*xx* account have permission to administer SQL Server? Explain.

    _____

    _____

    Does your Student*xx* account have permission to administer your partner's default instance of SQL Server?

    _____

    _____

▶   **To attach the Accounting database, grant database access to the Accounting group and the Smoky login account, create the Data Entry Managers role, and add the Smoky login account to that role**

1. In SQL Query Analyzer, click Connect on the File menu.

    The Connect To SQL Server dialog box appears.

2. In the Connect Using group box, click the Windows Authentication option button and then click OK.

    You are connected to SQL Server using your Student*xx* account. The membership of your Student*xx* account in the System Administrators role through the SQL Admins group takes effect when the new connection is made.

3. On the toolbar, click the Load SQL Script button.
4. Open Accounting.sql in the C:\Labfiles\Lab 10 folder.

Note If your \Labfiles folder isn't stored on drive C, replace C:\ with the correct drive letter. You also need to change the path in the Accounting.sql script.

A Transact-SQL script appears that will attach the Accounting database and grant the Accounting group and the Smoky login account access to that database. It also creates the Data Entry Managers user-defined database role in the Accounting database and adds the Smoky login to that role.

Note The Contoso\Accounting group contains the following Windows accounts: AccountingUser01 – AccountingUser12.

5. On the toolbar, click the Execute Query button to execute the Accounting.sql script.

   In the results pane, notice that the Account group was granted database access to the Accounting database and a new role was added.

6. Switch to SQL Server Enterprise Manager.

7. In the console tree, click the Databases container.

8. On the toolbar, click the Refresh button.

   The Accounting database now appears in the details pane.

9. In the console tree, expand the Databases container, expand the Accounting container, and then click Users.

   The users permitted access to this database appear in the details pane. Notice that the Contoso\Accounting group and Smoky appear as permitted users in this database, along with the dbo account.

   What users can access the Accounting database?

   _____

   How do members of the Accounting group have permission to log in to SQL Server?

   _____

10. In the console tree, click the Roles container.

    All the fixed database roles plus the user-defined Data Entry Managers role appear in the details pane.

11. In the details pane, double-click the Data Entry Managers role.

    The Database Role Properties – Data Entry Managers dialog box appears. Notice that Smoky appears as a member of that role. Notice that you can add only SQL Server logins.

12. Click the Cancel button.

Exercise 4
Viewing Access Information

In this exercise, you will use SQL Server Enterprise Manager and Transact-SQL system stored procedures to view SQL Server 2000 access information.

▶ **To view user access information using SQL Server Enterprise Manager**

1. In the console tree, in the Security container of the default instance click the Logins container.

   In the details pane, notice the Windows 2000 users and groups and the SQL Server logins that have access to SQL Server 2000. Notice that Contoso\ TestUser*xx* is denied access and the remaining accounts are granted access.

   How do you deny a SQL Server login access? Explain why it is different from denying a Windows user login access.

   _____

2. In the details pane, double-click Smoky.

   The SQL Server Login Properties – Smoky dialog box appears with the General tab selected. Notice that this is a SQL Server login.

3. Click the Server Roles tab.

   Notice that Smoky is a member of the Security Administrators server role.

4. Click Security Administrators, and then click Properties.

   The Server Role Properties – Securityadmin dialog box appears. Notice that Smoky is the only member of this server role.

5. Click the Permissions tab.

   What tasks can Smoky perform as a member of this server role?

   _____

   _____

   _____

6. Click Cancel to close the Server Role Properties – Securityadmin dialog box.

7. Click the Database Access tab.

   Notice that Smoky is a permitted user in the Accounting and NWCopy databases.

   What database roles does Smoky belong to in each database?

   _____

   _____

8. In the Specify Which Databases Can Be Accessed By This Login group box, click the Accounting database row. (Do not clear the check box for the Accounting database.)

9. In the Database Roles For Accounting group box, click Data Entry Managers and then click the Properties button.

   The Database Role Properties – Data Entry Managers dialog box appears. Notice that Smoky is the only member of this database role.

10. Click the Permissions button.

    The Database Role Properties – Accounting dialog box appears.

11. Click the List Only Objects With Permissions For This Role option button.

    Notice that no permissions have been granted to members of this database role. Permissions will be covered in detail in Chapter 11.

12. In the Database Role drop-down list, click Public.

    Notice that all permitted users in the Accounting database have select permissions on the system tables in the database but no permissions on any user tables.

13. Click Cancel to close the Database Role Properties – Accounting dialog box.

14. Click Cancel to close the Database Role Properties – Data Entry Managers dialog box.

15. Click Cancel to close the SQL Server Login Properties – Smoky dialog box.

▶ **To view database access information using SQL Server Enterprise Manager**

1. In the console tree, expand the Accounting container and then click the Users container.

   The users permitted access to this database appear in the details pane.

2. In the details pane, double-click Smoky.

   The Database User Properties – Smoky dialog box appears. Notice that this dialog box is the same as the one displayed in the previous procedure when viewing access information from the user perspective.

3. Click Cancel to close the Database User Properties – Smoky dialog box.

4. In the console tree, click the Roles container.

   The fixed and user-defined database roles appear in the details pane.

5. In the details pane, double-click Data Entry Managers.

   The Database Role Properties – Data Entry Managers dialog box appears. Notice this dialog box is the same as the one displayed in the previous procedure when viewing access information from the user perspective.

6. Click Cancel to close the Database Role Properties – Data Entry Managers dialog box.

7. Close SQL Server Enterprise Manager.

▶ **To view access information using Transact-SQL**

1. Switch to SQL Query Analyzer.

2. On the toolbar, click the Load SQL Script button.

   The Open Query File dialog box appears.

3. Open Logins.sql in the C:\Labfiles\Lab 10 folder.

Note If your \Labfiles folder isn't stored on drive C, replace C:\ with the correct drive letter.

A Transact-SQL script appears containing the sp_helplogins system stored procedure.

4. On the toolbar, click the Execute Query button to execute the Logins.sql script.

   In the results pane, notice two result sets. The first set displays the logins with access to this SQL Server 2000 instance. Notice that the logins for Contoso\ SQL Admins, Contoso\SQLService and Contoso\TestUser*xx* are not associated with a user name in any database. The second set displays the databases to which each login has access and the user name in the database.

5. On the toolbar, click the Load SQL Script button.

6. Open ServerRoleMembers.sql in the C:\Labfiles\Lab 10 folder.

Note If your \Labfiles folder isn't stored on drive C, replace C:\ with the correct drive letter.

A Transact-SQL script appears containing the sp_helpsrvrolemember system stored procedure. Three separate statements specify three separate server roles: the system administrator server role, the security administrator server role, and the server administrator server role.

7. On the toolbar, click the Execute Query button to execute the ServerRoleMembers.sql script.

   In the results pane, notice that the system administrator server role contains three members, the sa login account, the Contoso\SQL Admins group, and the Contoso\SQLService account. Notice that the security administrator server role contains only one user, Smoky, and the server administrator server role contains no users.

8. On the toolbar, click the Load SQL Script button.

   The Open Query File dialog box appears.

9. Open DatabaseAccess.sql in the C:\Labfiles\Lab 10 folder.

Note If your \Labfiles folder isn't stored on drive C, replace C:\ with the correct drive letter.

A Transact-SQL script appears, containing three system stored procedures that generate queries regarding the Accounting database. The sp_helpuser system stored procedure generates queries regarding the Contoso\Accounting Windows group. The sp_helprolemember system stored procedure generates queries regarding the Data Entry Managers user-defined database role. The sp_helpntgroup system stored procedure generates queries regarding all Windows groups with access to the current database.

10. On the toolbar, click the Execute Query button to execute the DatabaseAccess.sql script.

   In the results pane, notice that the Contoso\Accounting group is a member of the public role in this database. Also notice that Smoky is a member of the Data Entry Managers group. Also notice that the Contoso\Accounting group is the only Windows group with access to the Accounting database.

11. Close SQL Query Analyzer.

12. Log off your computer.

Lab 8: Managing SQL Server Permissions

Objectives

After completing this lab, you will be able to

- Grant statement permissions to users and groups
- Debug chain of object ownership issues
- Grant object permissions to users and groups
- Debug permission conflict problems
- Create and use application roles

Before You Begin

You must successfully complete Exercises 1 and 2 in Lab 1 and Exercises 1 and 2 in Lab 7 before you begin this lab. You also must create the \SQLBackups folder in Lab 6 on drive C (or on the drive where your SQL Server instances have been installed).

Note You must log on to your student computer using the correct domain user account to have sufficient permissions to perform the lab exercises in this Lab Manual.

Estimated time to complete this lab: 30 minutes

Exercise 1
Granting and Testing Statement Permissions

In this exercise, you will use SQL Server Enterprise Manager to grant CREATE VIEW and CREATE PROCEDURE permissions to the Data Entry Managers database role. Next, you will use Transact-SQL to grant BACKUP DATABASE and BACKUP LOG permissions to the Contoso\Accounting group. Then you will log on to Microsoft Windows 2000 as AccountingUser*xx* and use SQL Query Analyzer to attempt to create a view and a stored procedure while connected to Microsoft SQL Server as AccountingUser*xx*. You will also attempt to back up the Accounting database. Finally, you will log on to SQL Server as Smoky and attempt to create a view, a stored procedure, a table, and a database backup.

▶ **To connect to SQL Server with SQL Server Enterprise Manager**

1. Press Ctrl+Alt+Del to log on to the Contoso.msft domain.

   The Log On To Windows screen appears.

2. In the User Name text box, type **Student*xx*** (where *xx* is your computer number).

3. Verify that the Log On To text box displays Contoso. (If the Log On To text box does not appear, click the Options button.)

4. In the Password text box, type **password** and then click OK.

   Personal settings are applied, and you are logged on to Windows 2000.

5. Click Start, point to Programs, point to Microsoft SQL Server, and then click Enterprise Manager.

   SQL Server Enterprise Manager appears displaying the Microsoft SQL Servers and the Event Viewer (Local) console trees in the console root.

▶ **To grant CREATE VIEW and CREATE PROCEDURE permissions to the Data Entry Managers role using SQL Server Enterprise Manager**

1. In the console tree, expand the Microsoft SQL Servers container, expand the SQL Server Group container, expand the Server*xx* container (the default instance) and then click the Databases container.

   The databases for the default instance appear in the details pane.

2. In the details pane, right-click Accounting and then click Properties.

   The Accounting Properties dialog box appears.

3. Click the Permissions tab.

   The statement permissions for the Accounting database appear.

What users and groups currently have direct permissions to create database objects and perform backups?

_____

What users and groups currently have inherited permissions to create database objects and perform backups? Specify how each user or group inherited those permissions.

_____

4. Select the Data Entry Managers row, and then select the check box in both the Create View column and the Create SP column.

   Notice that you have granted two separate statement permissions to the Data Entry Managers database role.

   What database role could have been used to grant the permission to create views and stored procedures to the Data Entry Managers role?

   _____

   If that role had been used, what additional statement permissions would have been granted to the Data Entry Managers role?

   _____

   _____

   Since Smoky is the only member of the Data Entry Managers role, why were permissions not granted directly to Smoky?

   _____

   _____

   _____

   _____

5. Click OK to close the Accounting Properties dialog box.

▶ **To grant BACKUP DATABASE and BACKUP LOG permissions to the Contoso\Accounting group using Transact-SQL**

1. On the Tools menu, click SQL Query Analyzer.

   SQL Query Analyzer appears, and you are connected to SQL Server as Contoso\Student*xx*.

2. On the toolbar, click the Load SQL Script button.

   The Open Query File dialog box appears.

3. Open GrantBackup.sql in the C:\Labfiles\Lab 11 folder.

Note If your \Labfiles folder isn't stored on drive C, replace C:\ with the correct drive letter.

A Transact-SQL script appears that will grant the BACKUP DATABASE and BACKUP LOG statement permissions in the Accounting database to the Contoso\Accounting group.

Note The Contoso\Accounting group contains the following Windows accounts: AccountingUser01 – AccountingUser12.

4. Click the Execute Query button to execute the GrantBackup.sql script.

Notice that the BACKUP DATABASE and BACKUP LOG statement permissions are successfully granted.

5. Close SQL Query Analyzer and SQL Server Enterprise Manager.

6. Log off of Windows 2000.

► **To log in as AccountingUser*xx* and connect to SQL Server using SQL Query Analyzer**

1. Press Ctrl+Alt+Del to log on to the Contoso.msft domain.

The Log On To Windows screen appears.

2. In the User Name text box, type AccountingUser*xx* (where *xx* is your computer number).

3. Verify that the Log On To text box displays Contoso. (If the Log On To text box does not appear, click the Options button.)

4. In the Password text box, type **password** and then click OK.

Personal settings are applied, and you are logged on to Windows 2000.

5. Click Start, point to Programs, point to Microsoft SQL Server, and then click Query Analyzer.

The Connect To SQL Server dialog box appears.

6. In the Connect Using group box, click the Windows Authentication option button and then click OK to connect to the default instance of SQL Server.

SQL Query Analyzer appears, and you are connected to SQL Server as Contoso\AccountingUser*xx*.

► **To test statement permissions as AccountingUser*xx***

1. On the toolbar, click the Load SQL Script button.

The Open Query File dialog box appears.

2. Open Invoices.sql in the C:\Labfiles\Lab 11 folder.

Note If your \Labfiles folder isn't stored on drive C, replace C:\ with the correct drive letter.

A Transact-SQL script appears that will create the Invoices view in the Accounting database.

3. On the toolbar, click the Execute Query button to execute the Invoices.sql script.

Notice that AccountingUser*xx* does not have sufficient permissions to create a view in the Accounting database.

4. On the toolbar, click the Load SQL Script button.

The Open Query File dialog box appears.

5. Open YearlySales.sql in the C:\Labfiles\Lab 11 folder.

Note If your \Labfiles folder isn't stored on drive C, replace C:\ with the correct drive letter.

A Transact-SQL script appears that will create the Sales By Year stored procedure in the Accounting database.

6. On the toolbar, click the Execute Query button to execute the YearlySales.sql script.

Notice that AccountingUser*xx* does not have sufficient permissions to create a stored procedure in the Accounting database.

7. On the toolbar, click the Load SQL Script button.

The Open Query File dialog box appears.

8. Open Backup.sql in the C:\Labfiles\Lab 11 folder.

Note If your \Labfiles folder isn't stored on drive C, replace C:\ with the correct drive letter. Also, the backup path (\SQLBackups) in the Backup.sql script presumes that you created the \SQLBackups folder on drive C in Lab 6. If your path is different, change the pathname in the script accordingly.

A Transact-SQL script appears that will back up the Accounting database.

9. On the toolbar, click the Execute Query button to execute the Backup.sql script.

Notice that AccountingUser*xx* has sufficient permissions to back up the Accounting database.

10. On the File menu, click Disconnect.

▶ **To test statement permissions as Smoky**

1. On the File menu, click Connect.

   The Connect To SQL Server dialog box appears.

2. In the Connect Using group box, click the SQL Server Authentication option button.

3. In the Login Name text box, type **Smoky**.

4. In the Password text box, type **password** and then click OK to connect to the default instance of SQL Server.

   SQL Query Analyzer appears, and you are connected to SQL Server as Smoky.

5. On the toolbar, click the Load SQL Script button.

   The Open Query File dialog box appears.

6. Open Invoices.sql in the C:\Labfiles\Lab 11 folder.

Note If your \Labfiles folder isn't stored on drive C, replace C:\ with the correct drive letter.

A Transact-SQL script appears that will create the Invoices view in the Accounting database.

7. On the toolbar, click the Execute Query button to execute the Invoices.sql script.

   Notice that Smoky has sufficient permissions to create a view in the Accounting database.

8. On the toolbar, click the Load SQL Script button.

   The Open Query File dialog box appears.

9. Open YearlySales.sql in the C:\Labfiles\Lab 11 folder.

Note If your \Labfiles folder isn't stored on drive C, replace C:\ with the correct drive letter.

A Transact-SQL script appears that will create the Sales By Year stored procedure in the Accounting database.

10. On the toolbar, click the Execute Query button to execute the YearlySales.sql script.

   Notice that Smoky has sufficient permissions to create a stored procedure in the Accounting database.

11. On the toolbar, click the Load SQL Script button.

   The Open Query File dialog box appears.

12. Open CreateTable1.sql in the C:\Labfiles\Lab 11 folder.

Note If your \Labfiles folder isn't stored on drive C, replace C:\ with the correct drive letter.

A Transact-SQL script appears that will create Table1 in the Accounting database.

13. On the toolbar, click the Execute Query button to execute the Table1.sql script.

    Notice that Smoky does not have sufficient permissions to create a table in the Accounting database.

14. On the toolbar, click the Load SQL Script button.

    The Open Query File dialog box appears.

15. Open Backup.sql in the C:\Labfiles\Lab 11 folder.

Note If your \Labfiles folder isn't stored on drive C, replace C:\ with the correct drive letter. Also, the backup path (\SQLBackups) in the Backup.sql script presumes that you created the \SQLBackups folder on drive C in Lab 6. If your path is different, change the pathname in the script accordingly.

A Transact-SQL script appears that will back up the Accounting database.

16. On the toolbar, click the Execute Query button to execute the Backup.sql script.

    Notice that Smoky does not have sufficient permissions to back up the Accounting database.

17. Close SQL Query Analyzer.

18. Log off of Windows 2000.

Exercise 2
Granting and Testing Object Permissions

In this exercise, you will use SQL Server Enterprise Manager to grant SELECT permissions on the Invoices view to the public role and EXECUTE permissions on the Sales By Year stored procedure to the Data Entry Managers role. You will also grant DENY permissions on the Orders table. Next, you will add the Contoso\Accounting group to the Data Entry Managers role. Next, you will log on to Windows 2000 as AccountingUser*xx*. You will use SQL Query Analyzer to connect to SQL Server as Contoso\AccountingUser*xx*. You will then attempt to view data from the Orders table and the Invoices view, and attempt to execute the Sales By Year stored procedure. You will then connect to SQL Server as Smoky and attempt to view the Orders table and the Invoices view, and attempt to execute the Sales By Year stored procedure.

▶ **To connect to SQL Server with SQL Server Enterprise Manager**

1. Press Ctrl+Alt+Del to log on to the Contoso.msft domain.

   The Log On To Windows screen appears.

2. In the User Name text box, type **Student*xx***.

3. Verify that the Log On To text box displays Contoso. (If the Log On To text box does not appear, click the Options button.)

4. In the Password text box, type **password** and then click OK.

   Personal settings are applied, and you are logged on to Windows 2000.

5. Click Start, point to Programs, point to Microsoft SQL Server, and then click Enterprise Manager.

   SQL Server Enterprise Manager appears displaying the Microsoft SQL Servers and the Event Viewer (Local) console trees in the console root.

▶ **To grant the SELECT and EXECUTE object permissions using SQL Server Enterprise Manager**

1. In SQL Server Enterprise Manager console tree, expand the Microsoft SQL Servers container, expand the SQL Server Group container, expand the the default instance container, expand the Databases container, and then expand the Accounting database container.

2. Click the Views container.

   The views in the Accounting database appear in the details pane.

3. In the details pane, click the Name column to sort the views based on name.

   Notice that there are two views with the name of Invoices, one owned by Smoky and one owned by the dbo role.

Why are there two separate views with the same name?

_____

_____

_____

_____

_____

Could Smoky have specified dbo as the owner when the Invoices view was created?

_____

_____

_____

4. In the details pane, double-click the Invoices view owned by the dbo role.

   The View Properties – Invoices dialog box appears. Notice the Transact-SQL script for the view appears in the dialog box.

5. Click the Permissions button.

   The Object Properties – Accounting dialog box appears.

6. In the Public row, select the SELECT check box.

   Notice that the green check mark indicates that all members of the public role have SELECT permissions on the Invoices view.

7. Click OK to close the Object Properties – Accounting dialog box.

8. Click OK to close the View Properties – Invoices dialog box.

9. Click the Stored Procedures container.

   The stored procedures in the Accounting database appear in the details pane. Notice two stored procedures by the name of Sales By Year, one owned by the dbo role and one owned by Smoky.

10. In the details pane, double-click the Sales By Year stored procedure owned by the dbo role.

    The Stored Procedure Properties – Sales By Year dialog box appears. Notice that the Transact-SQL script for the stored procedure appears in the dialog box.

11. Click the Permissions button.

    The Object Properties – Accounting dialog box appears.

12. In the Data Entry Managers row, select the EXEC check box.

    Notice that the green check mark indicates that all members of the Data Entry Managers role have EXECUTE permissions on the Sales By Year stored procedure.

13. Click OK to close the Object Properties – Accounting dialog box.

14. Click OK to close the Stored Procedure Properties – Sales By Year dialog box.

▶ **To grant the DENY object permissions using SQL Server Enterprise Manager**

1. In the console tree, click the Tables container.

   The tables in the Accounting database appear in the details pane.

2. In the details pane, double-click the Orders table.

   The Table-Properties – Orders dialog box appears.

3. Click the Permissions button.

   The Object Properties – Accounting dialog box appears.

4. In the Public row, click the SELECT check box twice.

   Notice that the red X indicates that all members of the public role are denied SELECT permissions on this table.

5. Click OK to close the Object Properties – Accounting dialog box.

6. Click OK to close the Table Properties – Orders dialog box.

▶ **To add a Windows group to a database role using SQL Server Enterprise Manager**

1. In the console tree, click the Roles container.

   The database roles for the Accounting database appear in the details pane.

2. In the details pane, double-click Data Entry Managers.

   The Database Role Properties – Data Entry Managers dialog box appears. Notice that the only member is Smoky.

3. Click the Add button.

   The Add Role Members dialog box appears.

4. Click Contoso\Accounting, and then click OK.

   Notice that two users now appear as members of the Data Entry Managers role.

5. Click OK to close the Database Role Properties – Data Entry Managers dialog box.

6. Close SQL Server Enterprise Manager.

7. Log off Windows 2000.

   Does Contoso\AccountingUser*xx* have SELECT permissions on the Orders table in the Accounting database? Why or why not?

   _____

   _____

Does Contoso\AccountingUser*xx* have SELECT permissions on the Invoices view? Why or why not?

_____

_____

Does Contoso\AccountingUser*xx* have EXECUTE permissions on the Sales By Year stored procedure? Why or why not?

_____

_____

▶ **To log on as AccountingUser*xx* and connect to SQL Server using SQL Query Analyzer**

1. Press Ctrl+Alt+Del to log on to the Contoso.msft domain.

   The Log On To Windows screen appears.

2. In the User Name text box, type AccountingUser*xx*.

3. Verify that the Log On To text box displays Contoso. (If the Log On To text box does not appear, click the Options button.)

4. In the Password text box, type **password** and then click OK.

   Personal settings are applied, and you are logged on to Windows 2000.

5. Click Start, point to Programs, point to Microsoft SQL Server, and then click Query Analyzer.

   The Connect To SQL Server dialog box appears.

6. In the Connect Using group box, click the Windows Authentication option button and then click OK to connect to the default instance of SQL Server.

   SQL Query Analyzer appears, and you are connected to SQL Server as Contoso\AccountingUser*xx*.

▶ **To test object permissions as AccountingUser*xx***

1. On the toolbar, select Accounting from the drop-down list.

2. In the query pane, type **SELECT * FROM Orders** and then click the Execute Query button on the toolbar.

   Notice that SELECT permissions are denied on the Orders object owned by the dbo role in the Accounting database.

3. In the query pane, change the query to read **SELECT * FROM Invoices** and then click the Execute Query button on the toolbar.

   Notice that Contoso\AccountingUser*xx* has SELECT permissions on the Invoices object in the Accounting database owned by dbo.

4. In the query pane, change the query to read **SELECT * FROM Smoky.Invoices** and then click the Execute Query button on the toolbar.

   Notice that Contoso\AccountingUser*xx* does not have SELECT permissions on the Invoices object in the Accounting database owned by Smoky, nor on any of the underlying tables used by this Invoices view.

5. In the query pane, change the query to read **EXEC [Sales By Year] '7/10/1996' , '7/17/1996'** and then click the Execute Query button on the toolbar.

   Notice that Contoso\AccountingUser*xx* has EXECUTE permissions on the Sales by Year object in the Accounting database owned by dbo.

6. In the query pane, change the query to read **EXEC Smoky.[Sales By Year] '7/10/1996' , '7/17/1996'** and then click Execute Query on the toolbar.

   Notice that Contoso\AccountingUser*xx* does not have EXECUTE permissions on the Sales By Year object in the Accounting database owned by Smoky.

▶ **To test object permissions as Smoky**

1. On the File menu, click Disconnect.

   A SQL Query Analyzer dialog box appears asking whether you want to save any changes.

2. Click the No button.

3. On the File menu, click Connect.

   The Connect To SQL Server dialog box appears.

4. Click the SQL Server Authentication option button.

5. In the Login Name text box, type **Smoky**.

6. In the Password text box, type **password** and then click OK.

   You are connected to the default instance of SQL Server 2000 using the SQL Server login Smoky. Notice that the title bar indicates that you are connecting as Smoky.

7. On the toolbar, select Accounting from the drop-down list.

8. In the query pane, type **SELECT * FROM Orders** and then click the Execute Query button on the toolbar.

   Notice that SELECT permissions are denied on the Orders object owned by the dbo role in the Accounting database.

9. In the query pane, change the query to read **SELECT * FROM Invoices** and then click the Execute Query button on the toolbar.

   Notice that Smoky does not have permission on the underlying tables required by this view.

Why was Contoso\AccountingUser*xx* able to successfully execute the SELECT * FROM Invoices statement while Smoky is unable to successfully execute the identical statement?

_____

_____

_____

_____

10. In the query pane, change the query to read **SELECT * FROM dbo.Invoices** and then click the Execute Query button on the toolbar.

    Notice that Smoky has SELECT permissions on the Invoices object in the Accounting database owned by dbo.

    Why was Smoky able to successfully execute the SELECT * FROM dbo.Invoices statement to view data from the underlying tables while Smoky was unable to successfully execute the SELECT * FROM Invoices statement, given that Smoky had SELECT permissions on each different view?

    _____

    _____

    _____

    _____

11. In the query pane, change the query to read **EXEC dbo.[Sales By Year] '7/ 10/1996' , '7/17/1996'** and then click the Execute Query button on the toolbar.

    Notice that Smoky has EXECUTE permissions on the Sales By Year object in the Accounting database owned by dbo.

    Why was it necessary to qualify the ownership of the stored procedure when executed by Smoky and not when executed by Contoso\AccountingUser*xx*?

    _____

    _____

    _____

    _____

    _____

12. Close SQL Query Analyzer. Do not save any changes.

13. Close SQL Server Enterprise Manager and log off Windows 2000.

Exercise 3
Configuring and Testing Application Roles

In this exercise, you use SQL Server Enterprise Manager to create an application role and then grant permissions to the application role. You then use a Transact-SQL script to activate the application role and test permissions through the application role.

▶ **To connect to SQL Server with SQL Server Enterprise Manager**

1. Press Ctrl+Alt+Del to log on to the Contoso.msft domain.

   The Log On To Windows screen appears.

2. In the User Name text box, type **Studentxx**.

3. Verify that the Log On To text box displays Contoso. (If the Log On To text box does not appear, click the Options button.)

4. In the Password text box, type **password** and then click OK.

   Personal settings are applied, and you are logged on to Windows 2000.

5. Click Start, point to Programs, point to Microsoft SQL Server, and then click Enterprise Manager.

   SQL Server Enterprise Manager appears displaying the Microsoft SQL Servers and the Event Viewer (Local) console trees in the console root.

▶ **To create an application role**

1. In the console tree, expand the Microsoft SQL Servers container, expand the SQL Server group container, expand the default instance container, expand the Databases container, and then expand the Accounting database container.

2. Right-click the Roles container, and then click New Database Role.

   The Database Role Properties – New Role dialog box appears.

3. In the Name text box, type **AcctgAppRole**.

   Notice that the Permissions button is grayed. You cannot grant permissions while creating the database role.

4. Click the Application Role option button.

5. In the Password text box, type **pass** and then click OK.

   Notice that AcctgAppRole appears in the details pane with an application role type.

▶ **To grant permissions to the application role**

1. In the details pane, double-click AcctgAppRole.

   The Database Role Properties – AcctgAppRole dialog box appears. Notice that the Permissions button is active, but that you cannot add users to an application role.

2. Click the Permissions button.

   The Database Role Properties – Accounting dialog box appears with AcctgAppRole selected as the current database role.

3. For the Invoices view owned by the dbo role, select the SELECT check box to grant SELECT permissions on this view.

4. For the Orders table owned by the dbo role, select the SELECT check box to grant SELECT permissions on this table.

5. Click OK to close the Database Role Properties – Accounting dialog box.

6. Click OK to close the Database Role Properties – AcctgAppRole dialog box.

▶ **To activate the application role using Transact-SQL**

1. Click the Start button, point to Programs, point to Microsoft SQL Server, and then click Query Analyzer.

   The Connect To SQL Server dialog box appears.

2. In the Connect Using group box, click SQL Server Authentication.

3. In the Login Name text box, type **Smoky**.

4. In the Password text box, type **password** and then click OK.

   You are connected to SQL Server using the Smoky account.

5. On the toolbar, select the Accounting database from the drop-down list.

6. In the query pane, type **EXEC sp_setapprole 'AcctgAppRole' , {Encrypt N 'pass'} , 'odbc'** and then click the Execute Query button on the toolbar.

▶ **To test the application role**

1. On the toolbar, click the Clear Window button.

2. In the query pane, type **SELECT * FROM Orders** and then click the Execute Query button on the toolbar.

   Notice that SELECT permissions are denied on the Orders object owned by the dbo role in the Accounting database.

   Why was the application role denied SELECT permissions on the Orders object even though SELECT permissions were directly granted to AcctgAppRole?

   _____

   _____

   _____

   _____

3. In the query pane, change the query to read **SELECT * FROM Invoices** and then click the Execute Query button on the toolbar.

Notice that the application role has SELECT permissions on the Invoices object in the Accounting database owned by dbo.

Why was it not necessary to qualify ownership of the Invoices object?

_____

_____

_____

_____

4. In the query pane, change the query to read **SELECT * FROM Smoky.Invoices** and then click the Execute Query button on the toolbar.

Notice that AcctgAppRole does not have SELECT permissions on the Invoices object in the Accounting database owned by Smoky, nor on any of the underlying tables used by the Invoices view.

5. In the query pane, change the query to read **EXEC dbo.[Sales By Year] '7/10/1996' , '7/17/1996'** and then click the Execute Query button on the toolbar.

Notice that AcctgAppRole does not have EXECUTE permissions on the Sales By Year object in the Accounting database owned by dbo.

Why was AcctgAppRole unable to execute the Sales By Year stored procedure even though the Smoky has permission to execute the Sales By Year stored procedure?

_____

_____

_____

6. On the toolbar, click the Clear Window button.

7. In the query pane, type **SELECT * FROM Northwind.dbo.Customers** and then click the Execute Query button on the toolbar.

Notice the application role has SELECT permissions on the Customers table in the Northwind database.

Why does AcctgAppRole have SELECT permissions on the Customers table in the Northwind database?

_____

_____

_____

8. Close SQL Server Enterprise Manager and SQL Query Analyzer. Do not save any changes.

9. Log off your computer.

Lab 9: Performing Administrative Tasks

Objectives

After completing this lab, you will be able to

- Grant local administrator rights to the domain user account used for the Microsoft SQL Server and SQL Server Agent services
- Configure memory use by the SQL Server service
- Publish a SQL Server instance with Active Directory directory services
- Specify the CPU Idle condition for the SQL Server Agent
- Register a remote SQL Server instance
- Create a linked server configuration
- Configure XML Support in Internet Information Services (IIS)
- Configure SQL Mail and SQLAgentMail (optional lab)

Before You Begin

You must successfully complete Exercises 1 and 2 in Lab 1 and all exercises in Labs 7 and 8 before you begin this lab.

Note You must log on to your student computer using the correct domain user account to have sufficient permissions to perform the lab exercises in this Lab Manual.

Estimated time to complete this lab: 45 minutes

Exercise 1
Configuring the SQL Server and SQL Server Agent Services

In this exercise, you will grant local administrator rights to the SQL Server and SQL Agent Service domain user accounts. Next, you will use SQL Server Enterprise Manager and Transact-SQL to configure minimum and maximum memory parameters for the SQL Server service. You will then publish the default SQL Server instance to Active Directory directory services. Finally, you will specify the CPU Idle condition for the SQL Server Agent service.

▶   **To grant local administrator rights to the SQL Server and SQL Agent Service domain user accounts**

1. Press Ctrl+Alt+Del to log on to the Contoso.msft domain.

    The Log On To Windows screen appears.

2. In the User Name text box, type **Studentxx** (where *xx* is your computer number).

3. Verify that the Log On To text box displays Contoso. (If the Log On To text box does not appear, click the Options button.)

4. In the Password text box, type **password** and then click OK.

    Personal settings are applied, and you are logged on to Microsoft Windows 2000.

5. On the desktop, right-click the My Computer icon and then click Manage.

    The Computer Management MMC appears.

6. In the console tree, expand Local Users And Groups and then click Groups.

    The Built-in local groups on your computer appear in the details pane.

7. In the details pane, double-click Administrators.

    The Administrators Properties dialog box appears displaying the users and groups who are members of the local Administrators group. Notice your Studentxx account appears as a member of this group.

8. Click the Add button.

    The Select Users Or Groups dialog box appears. Notice that the text in the lower pane stating "<<Type Names Separated By Semicolons Or Choose From The List>>" is selected.

9. Type **Contoso\SQLService** and then click the Check Names button.

    Notice that the domain user account is verified and the name displayed changes to "SQLService (SQLService@Contoso)".

10. Click OK to close the Select Users Or Groups dialog box.

    Notice that Contoso\SQLService (SQLService@Contoso) appears in the list of members of the Administrators group.

11. Click OK to close the Administrators Properties dialog box.

12. Close the Computer Management MMC.

13. On the taskbar, right-click SQL Server Service Manager and then click MSSQLServer – Stop.

    A SQL Server Service Manager dialog box appears, asking whether you want to stop the MSSQLServer service on \\Server*xx*.

14. Click the Yes button.

    A SQL Server Service Manager dialog box appears, telling you that SQLServerAgent is dependent on MSSQLServer, and asks whether you are sure that you want to stop MSSQLServer and its dependent services.

15. Click the Yes button.

16. On the taskbar, right-click SQL Server Service Manager and then click MSSQLServer – Start.

    Why is it necessary to stop and restart the SQL Server service at this point?

    _____

    _____

    _____

▶ **To configure minimum and maximum memory parameters for the SQL Server service using SQL Server Enterprise Manager**

1. Click Start, point to Programs, point to Microsoft SQL Server, and then click Enterprise Manager.

    SQL Server Enterprise Manager appears, displaying the Microsoft SQL Servers and the Event Viewer (Local) console trees in the console root.

2. In the console tree, expand the Microsoft SQL Servers container and then expand the SQL Server Group container.

3. In the console tree, right-click the Server*xx* container (the default instance) and then click Properties.

    The SQL Server Properties (Configure) – Server*xx* dialog box appears.

4. In the Autostart Policies When The Operating System Starts group box, verify that the Autostart SQL Server, Autostart SQL Server Agent, and Autostart MSDTC check boxes are selected.

5. Click the Memory tab.

    What is the default memory configuration for the SQL Server service?

    _____

    _____

6. Set the minimum memory use to 32 MB.

7. Set the maximum memory use to 96 MB.

8. Click the Running Values option button.

   Notice that the memory configuration changes have not yet been applied.

9. Click the Configured Values option button, and then click OK to apply the memory configuration changes.

10. In the console tree, right-click the default instance container and then click Properties.

    The SQL Server Properties (Configure) – Server*xx* dialog box appears.

11. Click the Memory tab.

    Notice that the configured memory values are now 32 MB for the minimum memory and 96 MB for the maximum memory.

12. Click Cancel to close the SQL Server Properties (Configure) – Server*xx* dialog box.

▶   **To configure minimum and maximum memory parameters for the SQL Server service using Transact-SQL**

1. On the Tools menu, click SQL Query Analyzer.

   You are connected to SQL Server as Contoso\Student*xx*.

2. On the toolbar, click the Load SQL Query button.

   The Open Query File dialog box appears.

3. Open Memory.sql in the C:\Labfiles\Lab 12 folder.

Note If your \Labfiles folder isn't stored on drive C, replace C:\ with the correct drive letter.

A Transact-SQL script appears that will use the sp_configure system stored procedure to configure minimum and maximum memory parameters.

4. On the toolbar, click the Execute Query button to execute the Memory.sql script.

   In the results pane, notice that the originally configured memory values are displayed, followed by the newly configured memory values.

5. Click the Messages tab to view the DBCC messages related to the change of memory parameters.

   Notice that the RECONFIGURE statement was required to implement the change.

6. Close SQL Query Analyzer.

▶   **To publish the default SQL Server instance to Active Directory**

1. In the SQL Server Enterprise Manager console tree, right-click the default instance container and then click Properties.

The SQL Server Properties (Configure) – Server.xx dialog box appears.

2. Click the Active Directory tab.

3. Click the Add button.

   A SQL Server Enterprise Manager message box appears, indicating that the default SQL Server instance was published to Active Directory.

4. Click OK to close the SQL Server Enterprise Manager message box.

5. Click OK to close the SQL Server Properties (Configure) – Server.xx dialog box.

▶ **To specify the CPU Idle condition using SQL Server Enterprise Manager**

1. In the SQL Server Enterprise Manager console tree, expand the default instance container and then expand the Management container.

2. In the console tree, right-click SQL Server Agent and then click Properties.

   The SQL Server Agent Properties – Server.xx dialog box appears.

3. Click the Advanced tab.

4. In the Idle CPU Condition group box, select the The Computer Is Idle When check box.

   Notice the default parameters for the CPU Idle condition.

5. Click OK to close the SQL Server Agent Properties – Server.xx dialog box and accept the default parameters.

6. Do not close SQL Server Enterprise Manager.

Exercise 2
Configure a Linked Server

In this exercise, you will use SQL Server Enterprise Manager to register your partner's server. You will then establish a Service Principal Name (SPN) for the default SQL Server instance using the Setspn.exe Microsoft Windows 2000 Server Resource Kit tool. Next, you will set up your partner's server as a linked server using SQL Server Enterprise Manager. You will map local logins to remote logins using impersonation and delegation. You will then use Transact-SQL to test the linked server configuration.

▶ **To register your partner's default instance with SQL Server Enterprise Manager**

1. In the SQL Server Enterprise Manager console tree, right-click the SQL Server Group container and then click New SQL Server Registration.

   The Welcome To The Register SQL Server Wizard screen appears.

2. Select the From Now On, I Want To Perform This Task Without Using A Wizard check box, and then click Next.

   The Registered SQL Server Properties dialog box appears.

3. In the Server drop-down list, type **Serveryy** (where *yy* is your partner's computer number).

4. In the Connection group box, verify that the Use Windows Authentication option button is selected.

5. In the Options group box, clear the Show System Databases And System Objects check box and then click OK.

   Notice that your partner's server is successfully registered and appears in the console tree.

   Why do you have permission to register and administer the default instance on your partner's computer?

   _____

   _____

   _____

   _____

   _____

   Do you have permission to register and administer the named instance on your partner's computer?

   _____

   _____

   _____

Could you use the sa SQL Server login account to register and administer the named instance on your partner's computer?

_____

_____

_____

6. In the console tree, expand the default instance container for your partner's computer and then expand the Databases container.

   Notice that only user databases appear.

7. Close SQL Server Enterprise Manager, and then log off Windows 2000.

▶ **To establish an SPN for the default SQL Server instance**

1. Press Ctrl+Alt+Del to log on to the Contoso.msft domain.

   The Log On To Windows screen appears.

2. In the User Name text box, type **Administrator**.

3. Verify that the Log On To text box displays Contoso. (If the Log On To text box does not appear, click the Options button.)

4. In the Password text box, type **password** and then click OK.

   Personal settings are applied, and you are logged on to Windows 2000.

5. Click the Start button, point to Programs, point to Accessories, and then click Command Prompt.

   The Command Prompt window appears.

6. At the C:\> prompt, type **cd\labfiles\lab 12** and then press ENTER on your keyboard.

Note If your \Labfiles folder isn't stored on drive C, you need to switch to the correct drive letter before typing the cd command.

The current directory is changed.

7. At the C:\Labfiles\lab 12> prompt, type the following command (replacing the *xx* variable with your computer number) and then press ENTER.

   ```
   Setspn -a MSSQLSvc/Serverxx.Contoso.msft:1433 sqlservice
   ```

   The MSSQLSvc object is updating in the Active Directory database.

   Why was it necessary to log on to Windows 2000 as Administrator to run the Setspn utility?

   _____

   _____

8. When Setspn has finished (when the prompt reappears in the Command Prompt window), close the window and log off of Windows 2000.

▶ **To connect to SQL Server with SQL Server Enterprise Manager**

1. Press Ctrl+Alt+Del to log on to the Contoso.msft domain.

   The Log On To Windows screen appears.

2. In the User Name text box, type **Studentxx** (where *xx* is your computer number).

3. Verify that the Log On To text box displays Contoso. (If the Log On To text box does not appear, click the Options button.)

4. In the Password text box, type **password** and then click OK.

   Personal settings are applied, and you are logged on to Windows 2000.

5. Click Start, point to Programs, point to Microsoft SQL Server, and then click Enterprise Manager.

   SQL Server Enterprise Manager appears displaying the Microsoft SQL Servers and the Event Viewer (Local) console trees in the console root.

▶ **To set up your partner's server as a linked server**

1. In the console tree, expand the Microsoft SQL Servers container, expand the SQL Server Group container, expand the default instance container for your computer, and then expand the Security container.

Note Make sure you are administering your default instance rather than the default instance for your partner's computer.

---

2. In the console tree, right-click Linked Servers and then click New Linked Server.

   The Linked Server Properties – New Linked Server dialog box appears.

3. In the Linked Server text box, type **Serveryy** (where the variable *yy* is your partner's computer number).

4. In the Server Type group box, click the SQL Server option button.

5. Click the Security tab.

6. In the Local Login column, type **Smoky**.

7. In the Remote User column, type **sa**.

8. In the Remote Password column, type **password**.

9. In the For A Login Not Defined In The List Above, Connections Will group box, click the Be Made Using The Login's Current Security Context option button.

10. Click OK to close the Linked Server Properties – New Linked Server dialog box.

▶ **To test the linked server configuration**

1. On the Tools menu, click SQL Query Analyzer.

SQL Query Analyzer appears, and you are connected to SQL Server as Contoso\Student*xx*.

2. In the query pane, type the following query (replacing the *yy* variable with your partner's computer number).

```
SELECT * FROM Serveryy.Northwind.dbo.Customers
```

3. On the toolbar, click the Execute Query button.

   The contents of the Customers table from the Northwind database in the default instance of your partner's server are displayed.

4. On the File menu, click Connect.

   The Connect To SQL Server dialog box appears.

5. In the Connect Using group box, click the SQL Server Authentication option button.

6. In the Login Name box, type **Smoky**.

7. In the Password text box, type **password** and then click OK to connect to the default instance of SQL Server.

   SQL Query Analyzer appears, and you are connected to SQL Server as Smoky.

8. In the query pane, type the following query (replacing the *yy* variable with your partner's computer number).

```
SELECT * FROM Serveryy.Northwind.dbo.Customers
```

9. On the toolbar, click the Execute Query button.

   The contents of the Customers table from the Northwind database on the default instance of your partner's server are displayed.

▶ **To deny Smoky SELECT permissions and retest the linked server configuration**

1. Switch to SQL Server Enterprise Manager.

2. In the console tree, expand the default instance container on your partner's server, expand the Databases container, expand the Northwind database container, and then click the Users container.

   The permitted users appear in the details pane.

3. Right-click the Users container, and then click New Database User.

   The Database User Properties – New User dialog box appears.

4. In the Login Name text box, type **Smoky** and then click OK.

   Smoky appears in the list of permitted users shown in the details pane.

5. In the console tree, click the Tables container.

The user tables in the Northwind database are displayed in the details pane. Notice that no system tables are displayed. Also notice that no system databases are displayed in the console tree.

6. In the pane, right-click the Customers table and then click Properties.

   The Table Properties – Customers dialog box appears.

7. Click the Permissions button.

   The Object Properties – Northwind dialog box appears.

8. Click the SELECT check box for the user Smoky twice to deny SELECT permissions.

   Notice that a red X appears in the SELECT check box.

9. Click OK to close the Object Properties – Northwind dialog box.

10. Click OK to close the Table Properties – Customers dialog box.

11. Switch to SQL Query Analyzer.

    Your connection as Smoky to SQL Server appears.

12. On the toolbar, click the Execute Query button to re-execute the distributed query.

    The contents of the Customers table from the Northwind database on the default instance of your partner's server are displayed.

    Why was Smoky able to successfully query the Customers table on the default instance of your partner's server?

    _____

    _____

    _____

    _____

    _____

13. Switch to SQL Server Enterprise Manager.

14. In the console tree, expand the default instance container for your computer, expand the Security container, and then expand the Linked Servers container.

15. Right-click the Serveryy container, and then click Properties.

    The Linked Server Properties – Serveryy dialog box appears.

16. Click the Security tab.

17. Remove the mapping of the local login, Smoky, to the remote user, sa.

    Verify that the Be Made Using The Login's Current Security Context option button is selected.

18. Click OK to close the Linked Server Properties – Serveryy dialog box.

19. Switch to SQL Query Analyzer.

    Your connection as Smoky to SQL Server appears.

20. On the toolbar, click the Execute Query button to re-execute the distributed query.

    Notice that the SELECT permission is denied on the Customers object.

21. Close SQL Query Analyzer. Do not save any changes.

Exercise 3
Configuring XML Support in IIS

In this exercise, you will create an IIS virtual directory and configure access to SQL Server through the virtual directory. You will then query SQL Server using Internet Explorer.

▶ **To create an IIS virtual directory**

1. Using Windows Explorer, create a new folder called Northwind under C:\Inetpub.

Note If Windows 2000 Server wasn't installed on drive C, you might need to replace C:\ with the correct drive letter.

---

2. Close Windows Explorer.

3. Click Start, point to Programs, point to Microsoft SQL Server, and then click Configure SQL XML Support In IIS.

   The IIS Virtual Directory Management For SQL Server console appears, displaying a connection to your server.

4. In the console tree, expand your server, right-click Default Web Site, point to New, and then click Virtual Directory.

   The New Virtual Directory Properties dialog box appears with the General tab selected.

5. In the Virtual Directory Name text box, type **Northwind**.

6. In the Local Path text box, type **C:\Inetpub\Northwind**.

Note If Windows 2000 Server wasn't installed on drive C, you might need to replace C:\ with the correct drive letter.

---

7. Click the Security tab.

8. In the User Name text box, type **Smoky**.

9. In the Password text box, type **password**.

10. Verify that the SQL Server option button is selected, and then click the Data Source tab.

    A Confirm Password dialog box appears.

11. In the text box, type **password** and then click OK.

12. In the SQL Server text box, verify that (local) appears.

13. In the Database drop-down combo box, select Northwind.

14. Click the Settings tab.

15. Select the Allow URL Queries check box, and then confirm that the Allow Template Queries check box is selected.

16. Click the Virtual Names tab.

17. Click the New button.

    The Virtual Name Configuration dialog box appears.

18. In the Virtual Name text box, type **Queries**.

19. In the Type drop-down list, select Template.

20. In the Path text box, type **C:\Inetpub\Northwind** and then click the Save button.

Note If Windows 2000 Server wasn't installed on drive C, you might need to replace C:\ with the correct drive letter.

---

21. Click OK to create the new virtual directory.

22. In the IIS Virtual Directory Management For SQL Server console tree, click the Default Web Site container.

    Notice that the Northwind virtual directory appears in the details pane, configured for the Northwind database with a security access of Smoky.

23. Close the IIS Virtual Directory Management For SQL Server MMC.

▶ **To query SQL Server using Internet Explorer**

1. Using Notepad, open the XML Employee Query.txt file in the C:\Labfiles\Lab 12 folder.

Note If your \Labfiles folder isn't stored on drive C, replace C:\ with the correct drive letter.

---

2. Copy the HTTP query.

3. Open Internet Explorer.

    The Welcome To The Internet Connection Wizard screen appears.

4. Click Cancel.

    An Internet Connection Wizard dialog box appears, asking whether you are sure you want to close the wizard.

5. Select the Do Not Show The Internet Connection Wizard In The Future check box, and then click the Yes button.

    Internet Explorer appears, stating that the page cannot be displayed.

6. Paste the query to the Address drop-down combo box, and then click the Go button.

    The last names and home phone numbers from the Employees table in the Northwind database are displayed.

7. Using Notepad, open the XML Customer Query.txt file in the C:\Labfiles\Lab 12 folder.

Note If your \Labfiles folder isn't stored on drive C, replace C:\ with the correct drive letter.

---

8. Copy the HTTP query.

9. Paste the query to the Address drop-down combo box, and then click the Go button.

   Notice that you are unable to view the contact names and phone numbers from the Customers table in the Northwind database.

   Why were you unable to view the contact names and phone numbers from the Customers table in the Northwind database?

   _____

   _____

   _____

   _____

   _____

10. Switch to SQL Server Enterprise Manager.

11. In the Databases container for your default instance, expand the Northwind database container, and then click the Tables container.

    The system and user tables for the Northwind database appear in the details pane.

12. In the details pane, right-click the Customers table and then click Properties.

    The Table Properties – Customers dialog box appears.

13. Click the Permissions button.

    The Object Properties – Northwind dialog box appears. Notice the red X indicating Smoky is denied SELECT permissions on the Customers table.

14. Clear the SELECT check box for the user, Smoky.

15. Click OK to close the Object Properties – Northwind dialog box.

16. Click OK to close the Table Properties – Customers dialog box.

17. Switch to Internet Explorer.

18. On the toolbar, click the Refresh button.

    The contact names and phone numbers from the Customers table in the Northwind database are displayed.

19. Close SQL Server Enterprise Manager, Internet Explorer, and Notepad.

Exercise 4
Configuring the SQL Mail and SQLAgentMail (Optional)

In this optional exercise, you will install Microsoft Outlook on your computer and configure a messaging profile for your Student*xx* domain user account. Next, you will log on as SQLService and configure a message profile for this domain user account. Then, you will log back on as Student*xx* and use SQL Server Enterprise Manager to configure SQL Mail and SQLAgentMail to use the messaging profile created for the SQL Service Account.

▶ **To create a messaging profile for the Student*xx* domain user account**

1. On the desktop, double-click Microsoft Outlook.

   The Outlook 2000 Startup page appears.

2. Click Next.

   The E-mail Service Options page appears.

3. Click the Corporate Or Workgroup option button, and then click Next.

   After a few seconds, the Select The Information Service(s) That You Want To Use With Microsoft Outlook page appears.

4. In the Use The Following Information Services list box, select the Microsoft Exchange Server check box and then click Next.

   The Microsoft Outlook 2000 installation commences. The Please Enter Your Microsoft Exchange Server And Mailbox Name page appears.

5. In the Microsoft Exchange Server text box, type **Instructor01**.

6. Verify that the Mailbox text box displays Student*xx*, and then click Next.

   The Do You Travel With This Computer page appears.

7. Verify that the No option button is selected, and then click Next.

   The Done! page appears.

8. Click the Finish button.

   Microsoft Outlook appears. A Microsoft Outlook dialog box appears asking whether you would like to register Outlook as the default manager for Mail, News and Contacts.

9. Click the Yes button.

10. Close Microsoft Outlook.

11. Log off Windows 2000.

▶ **To create a messaging profile for the SQLService domain user account**

1. Press Ctrl+Alt+Del to log on to the Contoso.msft domain.

   The Log On To Windows screen appears.

2. In the User Name text box, type **SQLService**.

3. Verify that the Log On To text box displays Contoso. (If the Log On To text box does not appear, click the Options button.)

4. In the Password text box, type **sql** and then click OK.

   Personal settings are applied, and you are logged on to Windows 2000. The Microsoft Windows 2000 Configure Your Server screen appears.

5. Clear the Show This Screen At Startup check box, and then close the Microsoft Windows 2000 Configure Your Server screen.

6. On the desktop, double-click the Microsoft Outlook icon.

   Microsoft Outlook 2000 installation commences. The User Name dialog box appears.

7. Click OK to accept the default values.

   The Select The Information Service(s) That You Want To Use With Microsoft Outlook page appears.

8. Select the Microsoft Exchange Server check box, and then click Next.

   The Microsoft Outlook 2000 installation commences. The Please Enter Your Microsoft Exchange Server And Mailbox Name page appears.

9. In the Microsoft Exchange Server text box, type **Instructor01**.

10. Verify that the Mailbox text box displays SQLService, and then click Next.

    The Do You Travel With This Computer page appears.

11. Verify that the No option button is selected, and then click Next.

    The Done! page appears.

12. Click the Finish button.

    Microsoft Outlook appears. After a few seconds, a Microsoft Office 2000 Registration Wizard dialog box appears asking whether you would like to register your copy of Office 2000 with Microsoft.

13. Click the No button.

14. On the Tools menu, click Options.

    The Options dialog box appears with the General tab selected.

15. Click the Mail Services tab.

    Notice that the default profile name is MS Exchange Settings.

16. Click Cancel to close the Options dialog box.

17. Close Microsoft Outlook.

18. Log off Windows 2000.

▶ **To connect to SQL Server with SQL Server Enterprise Manager**

1. Press Ctrl+Alt+Del to log on to the Contoso.msft domain.

   The Log On To Windows screen appears.

2. In the User Name text box, type **Studentxx** (where *xx* is your computer number).

3. Verify that the Log On To text box displays Contoso. (If the Log On To text box does not appear, click the Options button.)

4. In the Password text box, type **password** and then click OK.

   Personal settings are applied, and you are logged on to Windows 2000.

5. Click Start, point to Programs, point to Microsoft SQL Server, and then click Enterprise Manager.

   SQL Server Enterprise Manager appears displaying the Microsoft SQL Servers and the Event Viewer (Local) console trees in the console root.

▶ **To configure SQL Mail to use the SQLService default messaging profile**

1. In the console tree, expand the Microsoft SQL Servers container, expand the SQL Server Group container, expand the default instance on your computer, and then expand the Support Services container.

2. In the Support Services container, right-click SQL Mail and then click Properties.

   The SQL Mail Configuration – Server*xx* dialog box appears.

3. Select MS Exchange Settings in the Profile Name drop-down combo box.

4. Click the Test Button.

   A SQL Mail Configuration – Server*xx* message box appears stating that a MAPI session was successfully started and stopped with this profile.

5. Click OK.

6. Click OK to close the SQL Mail Configuration – Server*xx* dialog box.

▶ **To configure SQLAgentMail to use the SQLService default messaging profile**

1. In the console tree, expand the Management container for the default instance.

2. In the Management container, right-click SQL Server Agent and then click Properties.

   The SQL Server Agent Properties – Server*xx* dialog box appears.

3. In the Mail Session group box, select MS Exchange Settings in the Mail Profile drop-down combo box.

4. Click the Test Button.

   A SQL Server Agent Properties – Server*xx* message box appears, stating that a MAPI session was successfully started and stopped with this profile.

5. Click OK.

6. Click OK to close the SQL Server Agent Properties – Server*xx* dialog box.

   A SQL Server Agent Properties – Server*xx* dialog box appears, telling you that changes will not take effect until SQL Server Agent is restarted and asks whether you want to start and stop SQL Server Agent now.

7. Click the Yes button.

▶ **To send a query result using SQL Mail**

1. On the Tools menu, click SQL Query Analyzer.

   SQL Query Analyzer appears, and you are connected to SQL Server as Contoso\Student*xx*.

2. On the toolbar, click the Load SQL Script button.

   The Open Query File dialog box appears.

3. Open SQLMail.sql in the C:\Labfiles\Lab 12 folder.

Note If your \Labfiles folder isn't stored on drive C, replace C:\ with the correct drive letter.

A Transact-SQL script appears that will execute a query that will determine the log space used by each database in this SQL Server instance and send the results to the Student*xx* mail account in the Contoso domain.

4. Change the *xx* variable in the SQLMail script to your computer number, and then click the Execute Query button to execute the SQLMail.sql script.

   Notice that the query executes successfully and the mail is sent.

5. On the taskbar, click the Launch Microsoft Outlook button.

   Microsoft Outlook appears displaying the contents of the Inbox. Notice that an e-mail has been delivered to your mailbox with the results of the query.

6. Select the mail received from the SQLService user, and then review the log space used by each database in this SQL Server instance.

7. Close Microsoft Outlook.

8. Close SQL Query Analyzer. Don't save any changes.

9. Close SQL Server Enterprise Manager.

10. Log off your computer.

Lab 10: Automating Administrative Tasks

Objectives

After completing this lab, you will be able to

- Create operators
- Create a fail-safe operator
- Create a multistep job
- Create an event alert
- Create a performance condition alert
- Define a master server, and enlist a target server
- Create a multiserver job

Before You Begin

You must successfully complete Exercises 1 and 2 in Lab 1 before you begin this lab. In addition, if you want to use SQLAgentMail, you must complete the optional Exercise 4 in Lab 9.

Note You must log on to your student computer using the correct domain user account to have sufficient permissions to perform the lab exercises in this Lab Manual.

Estimated time to complete this lab: 45 minutes

Exercise 1
Creating Operators

In this exercise, you will configure your partner and yourself as operators. In addition, you will configure your server as an operator. Next, you will configure yourself as the fail-safe operator.

▶ **To connect to SQL Server with SQL Server Enterprise Manager**

1. Press Ctrl+Alt+Del to log on to the Contoso.msft domain.

   The Log On To Windows screen appears.

2. In the User Name text box, type **Studentxx** (where *xx* is your computer number).

3. Verify that the Log On To text box displays Contoso. (If the Log On To text box does not appear, click the Options button.)

4. In the Password text box, type **password** and then click OK.

   Personal settings are applied, and you are logged on to Microsoft Windows 2000.

5. Click Start, point to Programs, point to Microsoft SQL Server, and then click Enterprise Manager.

   SQL Server Enterprise Manager appears, displaying the Microsoft SQL Servers and the Event Viewer (Local) console trees in the console root.

▶ **To create yourself as an operator**

1. In the console tree, expand the Microsoft SQL Servers container, expand the SQL Server Group container, expand the Serverxx container for your computer (the default instance), expand the Management container, and then expand the SQL Server Agent container.

2. In the console tree, right-click the Operators container and then click New Operator.

   The New Operator Properties – Serverxx dialog box appears.

3. In the Name text box, type **Studentxx** (where *xx* is your computer number).

4. In the E-Mail Name text box, type **Studentxx@Contoso.msft** (where *xx* is your computer number).

Note If you have installed Microsoft Outlook, you might want to click the Test button to verify that you can send this message and then verify that the message was received using Microsoft Outlook.

---

5. In the Pager E-Mail Name text box, type **Studentxx@Contoso.msft** (where *xx* is your computer number).

6. In the Net Send Address text box, type **Serverxx** (where *xx* is your computer number).

7. Click the Test button for the NET SEND address.

   A Test Net Send Address dialog box appears displaying a message stating that a network popup message will be sent to 'Serverxx'.

8. Click OK to send the message.

   A Messenger Service message box appears displaying a message from Serverxx to Serverxx testing the network pop-up notification.

9. Click OK to close the Messenger Service message box.

10. In the Pager On Duty Schedule group box, configure a pager on-duty schedule so that this operator will be on duty when you perform the remaining exercises in this chapter.

11. Click OK to close the New Operator Properties – Serverxx dialog box.

    In the details pane, notice that this operator is now displayed.

▶ **To create your partner as an operator**

1. In the SQL Server Enterprise Manager console tree for the default instance, right-click the Operators container and then click New Operator.

   The New Operator Properties – Serverxx dialog box appears.

2. In the Name text box, type **Studentyy** (where *yy* is your partner's computer number).

3. In the E-Mail Name text box, type **Studentyy@Contoso.msft** (where *yy* is your partner's computer number).

Note If you have installed Microsoft Outlook, you might want to click the Test button to verify that you can send this message and then have your partner verify that the message was received using Microsoft Outlook.

---

4. In the Pager E-Mail Name text box, type **Studentyy@Contoso.msft** (where *yy* is your partner's computer number).

5. In the Net Send Address text box, type **Serveryy** (where *yy* is your partner's computer number).

6. Click the Test button for the NET SEND address.

   A Messenger Service dialog box appears displaying a message stating that a network popup message will be sent to 'Serveryy'.

7. Click OK to send the message.

   A Messenger Service message box appears on your partner's computer, displaying a message from Serverxx to Serveryy testing the network pop-up notification. You might also receive a Messenger Service message box on your screen from Serveryy to Serverxx.

8. If the Messenger Service message box appears on your computer, click OK.

9. In the Pager On Duty Schedule group box, configure a pager on-duty schedule so that this operator will *not* be on duty when you perform the remaining exercises in this chapter.

10. Click OK to close the New Operator Properties – Server*xx* dialog box.

   In the details pane, notice that this operator is now displayed.

▶ **To designate yourself as the fail-safe operator**

1. In the SQL Server Enterprise Manager console tree for your default instance, right-click the SQL Server Agent container and then click Properties.

   The SQL Server Agent Properties – Server*xx* dialog box appears with the General tab selected.

2. Click the Alert System tab.

   Notice that no fail-safe operator has been designated.

3. In the Fail-Safe Operator group box, click Student*xx* in the Operator drop-down list.

   Notice Student*xx* is now the designated fail-safe operator. Also notice that the default notification method is by pager.

4. Select the E-Mail check box.

5. Select the Net Send check box.

   Notice that notification of the fail-safe operator will now be made using all available notification methods.

6. Click OK to close the SQL Server Agent Properties – Server*xx* dialog box.

Exercise 2
Creating a Multistep Job

In this exercise, you will use the Create Job wizard in SQL Server Enterprise Manager to create and schedule a database backup job. You will then use SQL Server Enterprise Manager to edit this job. You will change the owner of the job, add a second step to the job, and create a second schedule for this job. You will then test the execution of this job. You will then change the owner of the job and test the execution of the job again.

▶ **To create a backup job using the Create Job wizard**

1. In the SQL Server Enterprise Manager console tree, click any container within your default instance.

2. On the Tools menu, click Wizards.

   The Select Wizard dialog box appears.

3. Expand Management, and then double-click Create Job Wizard.

   The Welcome To The Create Job Wizard screen appears.

4. Click Next.

   The Select Job Command Type page appears.

5. Verify that the Transact-SQL Command option button is selected, and then click Next.

   The Enter Transact-SQL Statement page appears.

6. In the Database Name drop-down list, verify that master is selected.

7. In the Transact-SQL Statement pane, type the following script:

   ```
   BACKUP DATABASE master TO DISK = 'C:\masterDB.bak' WITH INIT
   ```

Note The path in the above Transact-SQL statement presumes that SQL Server 2000 is installed on drive C. If your path is different, change the path name in the statement accordingly.

---

8. Click the Parse button to verify the script.

   A Create Job Wizard message box appears stating that the job command parse succeeded.

9. Click OK.

10. Click Next.

    The Specify Job Schedule page appears.

11. Click the On A Recurring Basis option button.

12. Click the Schedule button.

    The Edit Recurring Job Schedule – Server*xx* dialog box appears.

13. In the Occurs group box, verify that the Weekly option button is selected.

14. In the Weekly group box, select the following check boxes: Mon, Tue, Wed, Thur, and Fri. Clear the Sat and Sun check boxes if they are selected.

    Notice that this schedule will execute this backup job every weekday at midnight beginning tonight and running indefinitely. No weekend backup schedule exists.

15. Click OK to close the Edit Recurring Job Schedule – Server*xx* dialog box.

    The Specify Job Schedule page reappears.

16. Click Next.

    The Job Notifications page appears.

17. In the Net Send drop-down list, click Student*xx* (where xx is your computer number).

18. In the E-Mail drop-down list, click Student*xx* (where xx is your computer number).

19. Click Next.

    The Completing The Create Job Wizard page appears. Notice that the details of this job are displayed in the description pane.

20. In the Job Name text box, type **master Database Backup** and then click the Finish button.

    A Create Job Wizard message box appears, stating that the job was created successfully.

21. Click OK to close the message box.

22. In the console tree, click the Jobs container.

    The master Database Backup job appears in the details pane. Notice that this job is enabled, runnable, and scheduled. Also notice that its next scheduled run time is midnight.

► **To modify the master Database Backup job**

1. In the details pane for the Jobs container, double-click the master Database Backup job.

    The Master Database Backup Properties – Server*xx* dialog box appears, displaying the properties of this job.

2. In the Owner drop-down list, click Contoso\SQLService.

3. Click the Steps tab.

    Notice that only a single step appears.

4. Click the New button.

   A New Job Step – Server*xx*\Master Database Backup dialog box appears.

5. In the Step Name text box, type **Copy Backup**.

6. In the Type drop-down list, click Operating System Command (CmdExec).

7. In the Command pane, type **Copy C:\masterDB.bak D:** .

Note The paths in the above Transact-SQL statement presume that SQL Server 2000 is installed on drive C, and that your second partition or drive is drive D. If your paths are different, change the path names in the statement accordingly.

This copy job step simulates copying a successful backup to a network share point for later archiving.

8. Click OK.

   Notice that two steps now appear for this job.

9. Double-click Step 1.

   The Edit Job Step – Server*xx*\Master Database Backup dialog box appears, displaying the details of this job step. Notice the BACKUP DATABASE statement from the first procedure.

10. Click the Advanced tab.

11. In the On Success / Failure Flow group box, select Goto Step: (2) Copy Backup in the On Success Action drop-down list.

    In what security context will this job step run? Why?

    _____

    _____

12. Click OK to close the Edit Job Step – Server*xx*\Master Database Backup dialog box.

13. Click the Schedules tab.

    Notice that the schedule you created in the previous procedure appears.

14. Click the New Schedule button.

    The New Job Schedule – Server*xx*\Master Database Backup dialog box appears.

15. In the Name text box, type **Weekend Schedule**.

16. In the Schedule Type group box, verify that the Recurring option button is selected and then click the Change button.

    The Edit Recurring Job Schedule – Server*xx* dialog box appears. Notice that the default schedule is weekly, on Sunday, at midnight.

17. Click OK to close the Edit Recurring Job Schedule – Server*xx* dialog box.

18. Click OK to close the New Job Schedule – Server*xx*\Master Database Backup dialog box.

    Notice that two schedules now appear for the master Database Backup job.

19. Click the Notifications tab.

20. Notice that the notifications you configured in the previous procedure appear. Also notice that, by default, the Windows application log records the failure of this job.

21. Click OK to close the Master Database Backup Properties – Server*xx* dialog box.

▶ **To execute the Backup master Database job manually**

1. In the details pane for the Jobs container, right-click the master Database Backup job and then click Start Job.

   The Start Job On Server*xx* dialog box appears, asking you which step you want to use to start the job execution.

2. Verify that Step 1 is selected, and then click the Start button.

   After a few moments, a Messenger Service message box appears, stating that the master Database Backup job succeeded and providing execution details about the job.

Note If you are using Microsoft Outlook, verify that you also received an e-mail informing you of the success of this job.

---

3. Click OK to close the message box.

4. In the details pane for the Jobs container, right-click the master Database Backup job and then click Refresh Job.

   In the details pane, notice that the Last Run Status column now displays information stating that the job executed successfully and specifies the date and time.

5. In the details pane for the Jobs container, right-click the master Database Backup job and then click View Job History.

   The Job History – Server*xx* dialog box appears. Notice that this job has been run once, was run successfully, e-mail and NET SEND notifications were sent, and the job was invoked by Contoso\Student*xx*.

6. Click the Show Step Details check box.

   Notice that Step 1 and step 2 (Copy Backup) now appear.

7. Click Step 1.

   Notice that the details of the backup database job step appear in the Errors And/Or Messages From The Job/Step Run At pane.

8. Click the Copy Backup step.

   Notice that the details of the Copy Backup file job step appear in the Errors And/Or Messages From The Job/Step Run At pane.

   What does the Process Exit Code 0 message indicate?

   _____

   _____

9. Click the Close button.

▶ **To change the owner of the Backup master Database job and then execute the job**

   1. In the details pane for the Jobs container, right-click the Backup master Database job and then click Properties.

      The Master Database Backup Properties – Server*xx* dialog box appears.

   2. In the Owner drop-down list, click Smoky.

   3. Click OK to close the Master Database Backup Properties – Server*xx* dialog box.

   4. In the details pane for the Jobs container, right-click the master Database Backup job and then click Start Job.

      The Start Job On Server*xx* dialog box appears asking you which step you want to use to start the job execution.

   5. Verify that Step 1 is selected, and then click the Start button.

      After a few moments, a Messenger Service message box appears, stating that the master Database Backup job failed and that the last step run was Step 1.

   Note If you are using Microsoft Outlook, verify that you also received an e-mail informing you of the failure of this job.

   Why did the job fail?

   _____

   _____

   6. Click OK to close the message box.

   7. In the details pane, right-click the master Database Backup job and then click View Job History.

      The Job History – Server*xx* dialog box appears, displaying information regarding the execution of the master Database Backup job. Notice that the most recent execution of the job appears at the top of the list and is highlighted.

   8. Select the Show Step Details check box.

Notice that only Step 1 appears. Step 2 (Copy Backup) was never executed because Step 1 was configured to quit reporting failure if Step 1 failed.

9. Click Step 1 for information about the most recent execution of the master Database Backup job.

   Notice that the reason this job step failed appears in the Errors And/Or Messages From The Job/Step Run At pane.

10. Click the Close button.

11. In the console tree, expand the Event Viewer (Local) container and then click the Application container.

12. In the details pane, double-click the error message that corresponds with the source, MSSQLServer.

   An Event Properties dialog box appears, displaying the details of the failed BACKUP DATABASE statement. Notice that no reason for the failure appears.

13. Click OK to close the Event Properties dialog box.

14. In the details pane, double-click the warning message that corresponds to the source, SQLServerAgent.

   An Event Properties dialog box appears displaying information about the failed job. Notice that no reason for the failure appears.

15. Click OK to close the Event Properties dialog box.

▶ **To grant Smoky permission to back up the master database and execute the job**

1. In the console tree, expand the Databases container for the default instance, expand the master database container, and then click the Users container.

   The permitted users in the master database appear in the details pane. Notice that Smoky is not a permitted user.

2. In the console tree, right-click Users and then click New Database User.

   A Database User Properties – New User dialog box appears.

3. In the Login Name drop-down combo box, click Smoky.

4. In the Database Role Membership group box, select the db_backupoperator check box and then click OK.

   Notice that Smoky now appears in the Users container for the master database.

5. In the console tree of the Management container for your default instance, click the Jobs container.

6. In the details pane for the Jobs container, right-click the master Database Backup job and then click Start Job.

   The Start Job On Serverxx dialog box appears, asking you which step you want to use to start the job execution.

7. Verify that Step 1 is selected, and then click the Start button.

   After a few moments, a Messenger Service message box appears stating that the master Database Backup job failed and that the last step run was step 2 (Copy Backup).

Note If you are using Microsoft Outlook, verify that you also received an e-mail informing you of the failure of this job.

   Why did the job fail?

   _____

   _____

8. Click OK to close the message box.

9. In the details pane, right-click the master Database Backup job and then click View Job History.

   The Job History – Server*xx* dialog box appears, displaying information regarding the execution of the master Database Backup job. Notice that the most recent execution of the job appears at the top of the list and is highlighted.

10. Select the Show Step Details check box.

    Notice that both Step 1 and step 2 (Copy Backup) appear. Step 1 executed successfully, and step 2 (Copy Backup) failed.

11. Click step 2 (Copy Backup) for the most recent execution of the master Database Backup job.

    Notice that the reason this job step failed appears in the Errors And/Or Messages From The Job/Step Run At pane.

12. Click the Close button.

▶ **To grant non-sysadmins permissions to run CmdExec jobs and execute the job**

1. In the console tree, right-click the SQL Server Agent container and then click Properties.

   The SQL Server Agent Properties – Server*xx* dialog box appears with the General tab selected.

2. Click the Job System tab.

   Notice that only users with sysadmin privileges can execute CmdExec and ActiveX Scripting jobs.

3. Clear the Only Users With SysAdmin Privileges Can Execute CmdExec And ActiveScripting Job Steps check box.

   The SQL Agent Proxy Account dialog box appears.

4. In the User Name text box, type **SQLService**.

5. In the Password text box, type **sql**.

6. In the Domain text box, type **Contoso**.

7. Click OK to close the SQL Agent Proxy Account dialog box.

   What rights will non-sysadmins have when executing operating system and Active Scripting jobs?

   _____

   _____

8. Click OK to close the SQL Server Agent Properties – Server*xx* dialog box.

9. In the console tree, click the Jobs container.

10. In the details pane for the Jobs container, right-click the master Database Backup job and then click Start Job.

    The Start Job On Server*xx* dialog box appears, asking you which step you want to use to start the job execution.

11. Verify that Step 1 is selected, and then click the Start button.

    After a few moments, a Messenger Service message box appears, stating that the master Database Backup job succeeded and providing execution details about the job.

Note If you are using Microsoft Outlook, verify that you also received an e-mail informing you of the success of this job.

---

12. Click OK to close the message box.

13. In the details pane, right-click the master Database Backup job and then click Refresh Job.

    Notice that the job now indicates that the most recent execution of the job was successful.

Exercise 3
Creating Alerts

In this exercise, you will configure an existing alert and specify an operator to be notified. You will then create a user-defined error message and use the Create Alert wizard to create an alert based on this error message. Next, you will test this alert by creating a stored procedure that raises this error message and then executing the stored procedure. This test will also test the fail-safe operator. You will then create a performance condition alert using SQL Server Enterprise Manager directly that will fire an alert, notify you, and back up the Northwind transaction log whenever it becomes 60% full. You will then test this alert by running a script to fill the transaction log.

▶ **To configure an existing alert**

1. In the SQL Server Enterprise Manager console tree, click the Alerts container in the SQL Server Agent container for your default instance.

   The nine demo alerts that ship with SQL Server 2000 appear in the details pane. Notice that each of these alerts are enabled and have never been fired.

2. In the details pane, double-click the Demo: Sev. 19 Errors alert.

   The Demo: Sev. 19 Errors Properties – Server*xx* dialog box appears with the General tab selected. Notice that this alert will fire whenever a severity 19 error occurs in any database.

3. Click the Response tab.

   Notice that no jobs are currently defined in response to this alert and no operators are currently designated to receive notification in the event this alert fires.

4. In the Operators To Notify group box, click the E-mail, Pager, and Net Send check boxes for the Student*xx* operator (where *xx* is your computer number).

   Notice that, by default, the alert error text is included only in e-mail and NET SEND messages. Also notice that the default delay between responses is 10 seconds.

5. Click OK to close the Demo: Sev. 19 Errors Properties – Server*xx* dialog box.

▶ **To create a user-defined error message**

1. In the console tree, right-click your default instance container, point to All Tasks, and then click Manage SQL Server Messages.

   The Manage SQL Server Messages – Server*xx* dialog box appears with the Search tab selected. Notice that you can search for existing messages by specified text, error number, and/or severity level.

2. Click the Messages tab.

3. Click the New button.

   A New SQL Server Message dialog box appears.

4. Verify that the Error Number spin box displays the number 50001.

   If the error number is not 50001, note the actual number.

5. Verify that the Severity drop-down list displays a severity level of 010 – Information.

6. In the Message Text pane, type the following text:

   ```
   The units in stock for %s has reached %d. Please reorder.
   ```

7. Select the Always Write To Windows Eventlog check box.

8. Click OK to close the New SQL Server Message dialog box.

   Notice that this error message appears on the Messages tab and a green check mark indicates that this message is logged.

   Why is it important that the error message be logged?

   _____

   _____

   _____

9. Click OK to close the Manage SQL Server Messages – Serverxx dialog box.

▶ **To create an alert for the user-defined error message**

1. On the Tools menu, click Wizards.

   The Select Wizard dialog box appears.

2. Expand Management, and then double-click Create Alert Wizard.

   The Welcome To The Create Alert Wizard screen appears.

3. Click Next.

   The Define The Alert page appears.

4. Click the Only If This Error Occurs option button.

5. In the Only If This Error Occurs text box, type **50001**.

   Notice that the Error Description text box displays the text of this message.

6. Click Next.

   The Specify A Database Or Error Keywords page appears.

7. In the Database Name drop-down list, click Northwind.

8. Click Next.

   The Define Alert Response page appears.

9. In the Notify Operator(s) group box, select the Pager check box for Student*yy* (where *yy* is your partner's computer number).

10. Click Next.

The Define Alert Notification Message page appears.

11. In the Alert Notification Message To Send To Operator pane, type **Reorder Needed**.

12. Select the Page check box to include this alert notification message in the pager notification.

13. Click Next.

The Completing The Create Alert Wizard page appears.

14. In the Alert Name text box, type Reorder Alert.

15. Click the Finish button.

A Create Alert Wizard message box appears stating the alert was created successfully.

16. Click OK to close the message box.

17. In the console tree of the SQL Server Agent container for your default instance, click the Alerts container.

In the details pane, notice that the Reorder Alert appears in the list of alerts.

▶ **To create a stored procedure and raise the user-defined error message**

1. On the Tools menu, click SQL Query Analyzer.

SQL Query Analyzer appears, and you are connected to SQL Server as Contoso\Student*xx*.

2. On the toolbar, click the Load SQL Script button.

The Open Query File dialog box appears.

3. Open Reorder.sql in the C:\Labfiles\Lab 13 folder.

Note If your \Labfiles folder isn't stored on drive C, replace C:\ with the correct drive letter.

A Transact-SQL script appears that will create a stored procedure that, when executed, will raise the user-defined error message defined in the previous procedure.

4. On the toolbar, click the Execute Query button to execute the Reorder.sql script.

Notice that the command completed successfully and that the stored procedure was created.

5. On the toolbar, click the Clear Window button.

6. In the query pane, type the following query:

```
USE Northwind

EXEC reorder @prodid = 2
```

7. On the toolbar, click the Execute Query button to execute the stored procedure.

   Notice that the stored procedure is executed. A Messenger Service message box appears, stating, "The units in stock for Chang has reached 25. Please reorder." Also notice that the comment, "Reorder Needed", appears in the error message. Finally, notice that the error message was sent to the fail-safe operator.

   Why was the error message sent to the fail-safe operator rather than Student*yy*?

   _____

   _____

   _____

8. Click OK to close the Messenger Service message box.

9. Close SQL Query Analyzer. Do not save any changes.

▶ **To create a performance condition alert**

1. In the console tree, right-click the Alerts container for your default instance and then click New Alert.

   A New Alert Properties – Server*xx* dialog box appears with the General tab selected.

2. In the Name text box, type **Northwind Log 60% Full**.

3. In the Type drop-down list, click SQL Server Performance Condition Alert.

4. In the Object drop-down list, click SQLServer:Databases.

5. In the Counter drop-down list, click Percent Log Used.

6. In the Instance drop-down list, click Northwind.

7. In the Alert If Counter drop-down list, click Rises Above.

8. In the Value text box, type **60**.

9. Click the Response tab.

10. Select the Execute Job check box, and then in the drop-down list, click (New Job).

    A New Job Properties – Server*xx* dialog box appears with the General tab selected.

11. In the Name text box, type **Nwind Log Backup**.

12. In the Owner drop-down list, click Contoso\SQLService.

13. Click the Steps tab.

14. Click the New button.

    A New Step – Server*xx* dialog box appears.

15. In the Step Name text box, type **Backup Step**.

16. Verify that the Type drop-down list displays Transact-SQL Script (TSQL).

17. In the Database drop-down list, click Northwind.

18. In the Command pane, type the following statement:

    ```
    BACKUP LOG Northwind TO DISK = 'C:\NwindLog.bak' WITH NOINIT
    ```

Note The path in the above Transact-SQL statement presumes that SQL Server 2000 is installed on drive C. If your path is different, change the path name in the statement accordingly.

---

19. Click the Parse button to test the syntax.

    A New Job Step – Server*xx* message box appears stating the parse succeeded.

20. Click OK to close the message box.

21. Click OK to close the New Job Step – Server*xx* dialog box.

22. Click the Notifications tab.

23. Select the Net Send Operator check box, click Student*xx* (where *xx* is your computer number) in the first drop-down list, and then click When The Job Completes in the second drop-down list.

24. Click OK to close the New Job Properties–Server*xx* dialog box.

    The New Alert Properties – Server*xx* dialog box re-appears with the Nwind Log Backup job selected.

25. In the Operators To Notify group box, select the E-mail and Net Send check boxes for Student*xx* (where *xx* is your computer number).

26. Click OK to create the alert.

    In the details pane, notice that the Northwind Log 60% Full alert appears in the list of alerts.

▶ **To change the recovery model for the Northwind database and back up the database**

1. In the console tree, expand the Databases container for your default instance.

2. Right-click the Northwind database container, and then click Properties.

    The Northwind Properties dialog box appears with the General tab selected.

3. Click the Options tab.

4. Notice that the default recovery model for the Northwind database is Simple.

5. In the Model drop-down list, click Bulk-Logged.

6. Click OK to close the Northwind Properties dialog box.

   Why is it necessary to change the recovery model of the Northwind database before testing the Northwind Log 60% Full alert?

   _____

   _____

   _____

   _____

7. In the console tree, right-click the Northwind database container, point to All Tasks, and then click Backup Database.

   The SQL Server Backup – Northwind dialog box appears.

8. In the Database drop-down list, verify that Northwind is selected.

9. In the Backup group box, verify that the Database – Complete option button is selected.

10. In the Destination group box, click the Add button.

    The Select Backup Destination dialog box appears.

11. In the File Name text box, type **C:\NwindDB.bak**.

Note The path named in step 11 presumes that SQL Server 2000 is installed on drive C. If your path is different, change the path name accordingly.

---

12. Click OK to close the Select Backup Destination dialog box.

13. Notice that C:\NwindDB.bak appears in the Destination group box.

14. Click OK to back up the Northwind database.

    A Backup Progess dialog box appears, and then a SQL Server Enterprise Manager message box appears stating that the backup operation has been completed successfully.

15. Click OK to close the message box.

    Why was it necessary to perform a complete database backup of the Northwind database before testing the Northwind Log 60% Full alert?

    _____

    _____

▶ **To open System Monitor and monitor the Percent Log Used counter**

1. Click Start, point to Programs, point to Administrative Tools, and then click Performance.

   The Performance console appears.

2. On the toolbar, click the Add button.

   The Add Counters dialog box appears.

3. In the Performance Object drop-down list, click SQLServer:Databases.

4. In the Select Counters From List list box, click Percent Log Used.

5. In the Select Instances From List list box, click Northwind.

6. Click the Add button, and then click the Close button.

   A chart displays the Percent Log Used counter for the Northwind database. Notice that the transaction log is almost 50% full.

▶ **To test the performance condition alert**

1. Switch to SQL Server Enterprise Manager.

2. On the Tools menu, click SQL Query Analyzer.

   SQL Query Analyzer appears, and you are connected to SQL Server as Contoso\Student*xx*.

3. On the toolbar, click the Load SQL Script button.

   The Open Query File dialog box appears.

4. Open TLogOverFlow.sql in the C:\Labfiles\Lab 13 folder.

Note If your \Labfiles folder isn't stored on drive C, replace C:\ with the correct drive letter.

A Transact-SQL script appears that will continually update the ContactName column in the Customer table in the Northwind database. Notice that a wait of 30 milliseconds has been specified. This is intended to prevent the transaction log from filling so quickly that the backup job does not have time to finish the back up before the transaction log file automatically grows.

5. On the toolbar, click the Execute Query button to execute the TLogOverFlow.sql script.

6. Switch to the Performance console.

   Notice that the transaction log begins to fill up. Several moments after the Percent Log Used counter exceeds 60 percent, a Messenger Service message box appears, stating that the Northwind Log 60% Full alert was fired and the Nwind Log Backup job was run.

7. Click OK to close the message box.

8. A Messenger Service message box appears stating the Nwind Log Backup job was successfully executed.

9. Click OK to close the message box.

10. Switch to SQL Query Analyzer, and then click the Cancel Query Execution button on the toolbar.

11. Close SQL Query Analyzer.

12. Close any open message boxes.

    In the Performance console, notice that the chart displaying the Percent Log Used counter in the Performance console indicates that the job has executed (that is, the transaction log was truncated).

13. Close the Performance console.

14. In the details pane for the Alerts container of your default instance, right-click the Northwind Log 60% Full alert and then click Refresh Alert.

    Notice that the Northwind Log 60% Full alert displays the last time the alert occurred, what notifications were sent, and how many times the alert was fired.

15. Right-click the Northwind Log 60% Full alert, and then click Properties.

    The Northwind Log 60% Full Properties – Server*xx* dialog box appears displaying the history of this alert.

16. Click the Reset Count button.

17. Click OK to close the Northwind Log 60% Full Properties – Server*xx* dialog box.

    Notice that the count in the Count column for Northwind Log 60% Full alert now indicates zero.

18. Do not close SQL Server Enterprise Manager.

Exercise 4
Creating a Multiserver Job

In this exercise, you will enable Mixed Mode authentication on your named instance and grant your partner sysadmin privileges on your named instance. You will then start the SQL Server Agent service on your default and your named instance. Next, you will designate your default instance of SQL Server as a master server and enlist the named instance on your partner's server as a target server. You will then create a multiserver job that will run on your partner's named instance. Finally, you will verify that the job was downloaded successfully to your partner's named instance and start the job remotely.

▶ **To enable Mixed Mode authentication for your named instance**

1. In the console tree, right-click the Server*xx*\Instance2 container (your named instance) and then click Properties.

   The SQL Server Properties (Configure) – Server*xx*\Instance 2 dialog box appears with the General tab selected.

2. Click the Security tab.

   Notice that the current authentication mode is Windows authentication.

3. Click the SQL Server And Windows option button, and then click OK.

   A SQL Server Enterprise Manager – Server*xx*\Instance2 dialog box appears, asking whether you want to restart the SQL Server service now.

4. Click the Yes button.

   A SQL Server Enterprise Manager dialog box appears, telling you that SQLAgent$Instance2 is dependent on MSSQLServer and will also be stopped. You are asked whether you are sure you want to stop MSSQLServer and its dependent services.

5. Click the Yes button.

   The SQL Server service is restarted.

▶ **To grant your partner sysadmin permissions on your named instance**

1. In the console tree, expand your named instance container and then expand the Security container.

2. In the console tree, right-click the Logins container and then click New Login.

   The SQL Server Login Properties – New Login dialog box appears.

3. In the Name text box, type **Student*yy*** (where *yy* is your partner's computer number).

4. In the Domain drop-down list, click Contoso.

5. Click the Server Roles tab.

6. Select the System Administrators check box.

7. Click OK to close the SQL Server Login Properties – New Login dialog box.

8. In the details pane for the Logins container, notice that your partner's domain user account appears as a permitted login.

▶ **To start the SQL Server Agent service on each of your SQL Server instances**

1. On the toolbar, double-click the SQL Server Service Manager icon.

   The SQL Server Service Manager dialog box appears.

2. In the Server drop-down list, verify that Server*xx* is displayed.

3. In the Services drop-down list, click SQL Server Agent.

4. Verify that the SQL Server Agent service is running. If not, click the Start/Continue button to start the SQL Server Agent service.

5. In the Server drop-down list, click Server*xx*\Instance2.

6. Click the Start/Continue button to start the SQL Server Agent service.

   After a few moments, the status line indicates the SQL Server Agent service has started on Server*xx*\Instance2.

7. Close SQL Server Service Manager.

▶ **To designate your default instance as a master server**

1. In the console tree, expand the Management container for your default instance.

2. In the console tree, right-click SQL Server Agent for your default instance, point to Multi Server Administration, and then click Make This A Master.

   The Welcome To The Make MSX Wizard screen appears.

3. Click Next.

   The Create 'MSXOperator' page appears.

4. In the E-Mail Address text box, type **Student*xx*@Contoso.msft** (where *xx* is your computer number).

5. In the Net Send Address text box, type **Server*xx*** (where *xx* is your computer number).

6. Click Next.

   The Select Servers To Enlist page appears. Notice that Server*yy*\Instance2 does not appear in the list of servers that can be enlisted as target servers because it has not been previously registered.

7. Click the Register Server button.

   The Register SQL Server Properties dialog box appears.

8. In the Server drop-down combo box, type **Server*yy*\Instance2** (where *yy* is your partner's computer number).

9. Verify that the Use Windows Authentication option button is selected in the Connection group box and then click OK.

   Notice that Server*yy*\Instance2 now appears in the list of servers that can be enlisted as target servers.

10. Select the Server*yy*\Instance2 check box, and then click Next.

    The Provide Target Server Description page appears.

11. Enter a description for the Server*yy*\Instance2 server into the Description cell, and then click Next.

    The Completing The Make MSX Wizard page appears.

12. Review the information, and then click the Finish button.

    A Make MSX Wizard message box appears stating that Server*xx* was successfully made an MSX.

13. Click OK to close the message box.

    In the console tree, notice that the SQL Server Agent container for your default instance is designated as an MSX.

14. In the console tree, expand the Server*yy*\Instance2 container and then expand the Management container.

    Notice that the SQL Server Agent container for Server*yy*\Instance2 is designated as a TSX. Notice that it also lists the instance that is functioning as the master server.

▶   **To create a multiserver job**

1. In the console tree, expand the SQL Server Agent container for your default instance, and then expand the Jobs container.

2. In the console tree, right-click Multi Server Jobs, and then click New Job.

   The New Job Properties – Server*xx* dialog box appears.

3. In the Name text box, type **Backup All master Databases**.

4. In the Owner drop-down list, click Contoso\SQLService.

5. Click the Change button.

   The Change Job Target Servers – Server*xx* dialog box appears.

6. Click the right-arrow button to select Server*yy*\Instance2 as a target server for this new job, and then click OK.

7. Click the Steps tab, and then click the New button.

   The New Job Step – Server*xx* dialog box appears.

8. In the Step Name text box, type **Backup master Step**.

9. Verify that the Type drop-down list displays Transact-SQL Script (TSQL) and the Database drop-down list displays the master.

10. In the Command pane, type the following command:

```
BACKUP DATABASE master TO DISK='C:\master.bak'
```

Note The path in the above Transact-SQL statement presumes that SQL Server 2000 is installed on drive C. If your path is different, change the path name in the statement accordingly.

---

11. Click the Parse button to verify the script.

   A New Job Step - Server*xx* message box appears stating that the parse succeeded.

12. Click OK.

13. Click OK to close the New Job Step – Server*xx* dialog box.

14. Click the Schedules tab, and then click the New Schedule button.

   The New Job Schedule – Server*xx* dialog box appears.

15. In the Name text box, type **Nightly Schedule**.

16. Click the Change button.

   The Edit Recurring Job Schedule – Server*xx* dialog box appears.

17. In the Occurs group box, click the Daily option button, and then click OK to close the Edit Recurring Job Schedule – Server*xx* dialog box.

18. Click OK to close the New Job Schedule – Server*xx* dialog box.

19. Click the Notifications tab.

20. Select the Net Send Operator check box, verify that MSXOperator is selected in the first Net Send Operator drop-down list, and then click Whenever The Job Completes in the Net Send Operator second drop-down list.

21. Click OK to close the New Job Properties – Server*xx* dialog box.

   In the details pane, notice the new multiserver job. After 10 or 15 seconds, the Pending Instructions column will indicate zero. This means that the target server has downloaded the job. You might need to refresh the job by right-clicking the Backup All master Databases job in the details pane and then clicking Refresh Job to refresh the display.

▶ **To review the multiserver job on the target server**

1. In the console tree, expand the Server*yy*\Instance2 container, expand the Management container, expand the SQL Server Agent (TSX: Server*yy*) container, and then click Jobs.

   In the details pane, notice that the Backup All master Databases job appears.

2. In the details pane, right-click the Backup All master Databases job, and then click Properties.

   The Backup All Master Databases Properties – Server*yy*\Instance2 dialog box appears with the General tab selected.

3. Click the Steps tab.

   Notice that you cannot edit the job steps on a target server because the New, Insert, and Delete buttons are grayed.

4. Click the View button.

   The View Job Step – Server*yy*\Instance2\Backup All Master Databases dialog box appears displaying the details of the job step.

5. Click the Close button to close the View Job Step – Server*yy*\Instance2\Backup All Master Databases dialog box.

6. Click the Schedules tab.

   Notice that you cannot edit the schedule on a target server.

7. Click the Close button to close the Backup All Master Databases Properties – Server*yy*\Instance2 dialog box.

▶ **To start the job on the target server manually**

1. In the console tree Management container for your default instance, expand the SQL Server Agent container, expand the Jobs container, and then click the Multi Server Jobs container.

   The Backup All master Databases job appears in the details pane.

2. In the details pane, right-click Backup All master Databases, point to Start Job, and then click Start On All Targeted Servers.

   Notice that the Pending Instructions column indicates one pending instruction. After 10 to 15 seconds, the instruction will be downloaded and after several more moments a Messenger Service message box appears, indicating that the Backup All master Databases job was run on the target server.

3. Click OK to close the message box.

▶ **To view target server and job history information**

1. In the details pane, right-click Backup All master Databases, and then click Job Status.

   The Multi Server Job Execution Status – Server*xx* dialog box appears, displaying information regarding the Backup All master Databases job and each target server. Notice that you can view multiserver information by job or by server.

2. Click the View Remote Job History button.

   The Job History – Server*yy*\Instance2 dialog box appears. Notice that the information displayed from the remote server regarding the job is the same information that appears when reviewing the job history log for a local job.

3. Click the Close button to close the Job History – Server*yy*\Instance2 dialog box.

4. Click the Target Servers Status button.

   The Target Servers – Server*xx* dialog box appears, displaying information regarding each target server, its local time, last poll time, number of unread instructions, and status.

5. Click the Post Instructions button.

   The Post Download Instructions – Server*xx* dialog box appears.

6. In the Instruction Type drop-down list, click Synchronize Clocks and then click OK.

   A Post Download Instructions – Server*xx* message box appears, stating that 1 clock-synchronization request was successfully posted.

7. Click OK to close the message box.

8. Click the Download Instructions tab.

   Each of the instructions downloaded to the target server are displayed. Three instructions should appear: one for the download of the job to the target server, one to start the job on the target server, and one to synchronize the clock on the target server. If all three instructions do not appear immediately, click the Refresh button.

9. Click the Close button to close the Target Servers – Server*xx* dialog box.

10. Click the Close button to close the Multi Server Job Execution Status – Server*xx* dialog box.

11. In the details pane, right-click the Backup All master Databases job and then click Refresh Job.

    The Pending Instructions column now indicates zero pending instructions.

12. Close SQL Server Enterprise Manager.

13. Log off your computer.

Lab 11: Monitoring SQL Server Performance and Activity

Objectives

After completing this lab, you will be able to

- Monitor resource use using System Monitor, Task Manager, and Transact-SQL
- Monitor SQL events for performance using SQL Profiler
- Monitor SQL events for user activity using SQL Profiler
- Monitor SQL Server for blocking locks using the Current Activity Window and Transact-SQL

Before You Begin

You must successfully complete Exercises 1 and 2 in Lab 1 before you begin this lab.

Note You must log on to your student computer using the correct domain user account to have sufficient permissions to perform the lab exercises in this Lab Manual.

Estimated time to complete this lab: 45 minutes

Exercise 1
Monitoring Resource Use with System Monitor and Task Manager

In this exercise, you will monitor use of memory, processor, and disk resources using System Monitor and Task Manager.

▶ **To log on and configure Task Manager**

1. Press Ctrl+Alt+Del to log on to the Contoso.msft domain.

   The Log On To Windows screen appears.

2. In the User Name text box, type **Studentxx** (where *xx* is your computer number).

3. Verify that the Log On To text box displays Contoso. (If the Log On To text box does not appear, click the Options button.)

4. In the Password text box, type **password** and then click OK.

   Personal settings are applied, and you are logged on to Microsoft Windows 2000.

5. Right-click the Windows taskbar, and then click Task Manager.

   Windows Task Manager appears.

6. Click the Performance tab.

   Notice the overall values for process and memory use.

7. Is the Available Physical Memory (K) counter greater than 10 MB? What is the significance of this value?

   _____

   _____

   _____

   Is the Peak Commit Charge (K) value greater than the Total Physical Memory (K) value? What is this significance of a Commit Charge (K) value that is greater than the Total Physical Memory (K) value?

   _____

   _____

   _____

   _____

   _____

Why is the Limit Commit Charge (K) value greater than the Total Physical Memory (K) value?

_____

_____

_____

_____

_____

8. Click the Processes tab.

   Notice the five default columns.

9. Click the Image Name column to sort the column alphabetically.

   Notice that there are two instances of Sqlservr.exe currently running.

10. On the taskbar, double-click the SQL Server Service Manager icon.

    The SQL Server Service Manager dialog box appears.

11. In the Server drop-down list, click Server*xx*\Instance2.

12. In the Services drop-down list, click SQL Server.

13. Click the Stop button.

14. A SQL Server Service Manager dialog box appears, asking whether you want to stop the MSSQL$Instance2 service on Server*xx*.

15. Click the Yes button.

    A SQL Server Service Manager dialog box appears, informing you that the SQLAgent$Instance2 service will also be stopped and asking whether you are sure this is what you want to do.

16. Click the Yes button.

17. Close the SQL Server Service Manager application.

    Notice that only one instance of the Sqlservr.exe application remains.

18. Click the View menu, and then click Select Columns.

    The Select Columns dialog box appears, displaying a list of additional columns that can be selected.

19. Select the check boxes for each of the following columns. (Do not clear any of the check boxes that are already selected):

    - Peak Memory Usage
    - Page Faults
    - I/O Reads
    - Virtual Memory Size
    - Thread Count
    - I/O Writes

20. Click OK to close the Select Columns dialog box, and then expand Windows Task Manager.

    The additional columns are displayed.

21. Move the MemUsage column and the Peak Mem Usage column next to the Image Name column.

22. Click Sqlservr.exe in the Image Name column.

    Notice the current values for this SQL Server instance. Current memory usage, displayed in the Mem Usage column, should be approximately 14092 K, and CPU usage, displayed in the CPU column, should be approximately zero.

23. On the Options menu, click Hide When Minimized and then minimize Windows Task Manager.

    Notice that a Task Manager icon displaying CPU Usage appears on the system tray. Also notice that the current processor activity is essentially zero.

▶   **To load and review a saved System Monitor configuration**

1. Click the Start button, and then click Run.

    The Run dialog box appears.

2. In the Open text box, type **C:\Labfiles\Lab 14\Perfmon.msc** and then click OK.

Note If your \Labfiles folder isn't stored on drive C, replace C:\ with the correct drive letter.

A preconfigured System Monitor management console (entitled Performance) appears in Report view. Notice that a variety of counters are already loaded. Review the values for the various counters.

What is the current Processor Queue Length value for the System performance object?

---

3. On the toolbar, click the Freeze Display button.

4. Click the Start button, and then click Run.

    The Run dialog box appears.

5. In the Open text box, type **C:\Labfiles\Lab 14\Perfmon.msc** and then click OK.

Note If your \Labfiles folder isn't stored on drive C, replace C:\ with the correct drive letter.

A second version of the same preconfigured System Monitor management console (entitled Performance) appears in Report view.

6. Right-click the taskbar, and then click Tile Windows Vertically.

The two Performance consoles are displayed side by side.

▶ **To use a Transact-SQL script to place a load on SQL Server**

1. Click the Start button, point to Programs, point to Microsoft SQL Server, and then click Query Analyzer.

The Connect To SQL Server dialog box appears.

2. Click the Windows Authentication option button, and then click OK.

3. On the toolbar, click the Load SQL Script button.

The Open Query File dialog box appears.

4. Open LoadInLoop.sql in the C:\Labfiles\Lab 14 folder.

Note If your \Labfiles folder isn't stored on drive C, replace C:\ with the correct drive letter.

A Transact-SQL script appears that will run in a loop and execute a variety of Transact-SQL statements to place a load on SQL Server for you to monitor. Notice also that a slight delay has been placed between statements to avoid overloading your computer. Modify the delay if needed to increase or decrease the load on your computer.

5. On the toolbar, click the Execute Query button to execute the LoadInLoop.sql script.

Notice that the script begins to execute.

▶ **To analyze the load placed on SQL Server and on your hardware resources**

1. Minimize SQL Query Analyzer.

The two System Monitor windows appear. In one, the display is frozen. In the other, you can view the current load on the system.

What is the current value for the Processor Queue Length counter for the System performance object? What does this value indicate with respect to SQL Server performance?

_____

_____

_____

What is the current value for the %Processor Time counter for the Processor performance object?

_____

_____

What is the current value for the %Processor Time counter for the Process performance object for the Sqlservr instance and the Isqlw instance (Isqlw = SQL Query Analyzer)? What does the value observed mean with respect to your computer.

_____

_____

_____

Compare the current value for the Total Server Memory (KB) counter for the SQLServer:Memory Manager performance object with the value for this counter before the load was placed on SQL Server. What is the significance of the difference between these two values?

_____

_____

Compare the current value for the various counters for the PhysicalDisk performance object with the value for these counters before the load was placed on SQL Server. Is the disk subsystem a bottleneck given this load on the system? Which counter is most useful in answering this question?

_____

_____

_____

What type of disk activity is predominating given this set of queries?

_____

_____

_____

2. In the system tray, notice the level of processor activity displayed in the Task Manager icon and then double-click the Task Manager icon.

   Windows Task Manager appears with the Processes tab selected.

3. Click the Mem Usage column to sort this column hierarchically.

   Which process is currently consuming the greatest amount of memory?

_____

4. Click the CPU column to sort this column hierarchically.

   Which process is currently consuming the greatest percentage of processor time?

   _____

5. Close Windows Task Manager.

6. Close both System Monitor management console windows.

   A Microsoft Management Console dialog box might appear for each console window asking whether you want to save console settings to Perfmon.msc.

7. Click the No button.

8. Switch to SQL Query Analyzer.

   Notice that the script continues to run.

9. On the toolbar, click the Cancel Query Execution button.

   After several moments, the script will stop running. The slower your computer, the longer it will take for this script to stop running. It might take more than 60 seconds on slower computers.

10. Do not close SQL Query Analyzer.

Exercise 2
Monitoring SQL Events Using SQL Profiler

In this exercise, you will use SQL Profiler to trace SQL events based on performance and based on user activity.

▶ **To start a performance monitoring trace using SQL Profiler**

1. Click Start, point to Programs, point to Microsoft SQL Server, and then click Profiler.

    SQL Profiler appears.

2. On the toolbar, click the New Trace button.

    The Connect To SQL Server dialog box appears.

3. Make sure that the Windows Authentication option button is selected, and then click OK to connect to Server*xx* (the default instance).

    The Trace Properties dialog box appears.

4. In the Trace Name text box, type **Duration**.

5. In the Template Name drop-down list, click SQLProfilerTSQL_Duration and then click the Events tab.

    Notice that the only event classes being traced are RPC:Completed and SQL:BatchCompleted.

6. Click the Data Columns tab.

    Notice that the data columns selected are being grouped by EventClass and then by Duration.

7. Click the Filters tab.

    Notice that events generated by SQL Profiler are being excluded.

8. Expand DatabaseName, and then expand Like.

9. Type **Northwind** in the Like text box.

10. Expand Duration, and then expand Greater Than Or Equal.

11. Type **100** in the Greater Than Or Equal text box.

12. Expand NTUserName, and then expand Not Like.

13. Type **SQLService** in the Not Like text box.

14. Click the Run button.

    Notice that the Duration trace starts.

▶ **To start a user activity trace using SQL Profiler**

1. On the toolbar, click the New Trace button.

    The Connect To SQL Server dialog box appears.

2. Make sure that the Windows Authentication option button is selected, and then click OK to connect to your default instance.

   The Trace Properties dialog box appears.

3. In the Trace Name text box, type **User Activity**.

4. In the Template Name drop-down list, verify that SQLProfilerStandard is selected and then click the Events tab.

   Notice that the event classes being traced are Audit Logon and Audit Logout, Existing Connnections, RPC:Completed, and SQL: BatchCompleted.

5. Click the Data Columns tab.

   Notice that the data columns selected are not being grouped.

6. In the Selected Data list box, click NTUserName and then click the Up button several times to place NTUserName under Groups.

7. Click the Filters tab.

   Notice that events generated by SQL Profiler are being excluded.

8. Expand NTUserName, and then expand Not Like.

9. Type **SQLService** in the Not Like text box.

10. Expand Like.

11. Type **Studentxx** in the Like text box (where *xx* is your computer number).

12. Click the Run button.

    Notice that the User Activity trace starts.

▶ **To execute the Load script to generate data to analyze with SQL Profiler**

1. Switch to SQL Query Analyzer.

2. On the toolbar, click the Load SQL Script button.

   The Open Query File dialog box appears.

3. Open Load.sql in the C:\Labfiles\Lab 14 folder.

Note If your \Labfiles folder isn't stored on drive C, replace C:\ with the correct drive letter.

A Transact-SQL script appears that performs a variety of SELECT statements, which will take differing amounts of time to complete. These are the same scripts that were executed in a loop in the previous exercise.

4. On the toolbar, click the Execute Query button to run the Load.sql. script.

5. After the query completes, minimize SQL Query Analyzer. Do not close SQL Query Analyzer.

▶ **To analyze the Duration trace**

1. On the SQL Profiler toolbar, click the Stop Selected Trace button to stop the User Activity trace.

2. Click the Duration trace in SQL Profiler and then, on the SQL Profiler toolbar, click the Stop Selected Trace button to stop the Duration trace.

   Notice that the Duration trace displays the length of time required to execute each of the separate SQL batches and displays the text data for each batch in the Text Data column.

3. In the Duration trace, click the SQL batch containing the SELECT statement that took the longest to execute.

   Notice that the actual Transact-SQL script executed by this SQL batch is displayed in the lower pane.

   Do you have enough information to determine whether this query is inefficient?

   _____

4. In the lower pane, copy the entire text of this long-running query by highlighting the text and then pressing Ctrl+C.

5. Switch to SQL Query Analyzer.

6. On the toolbar, click the Clear Window button.

7. Right-click within the query pane, and then click Paste.

   The longest-running query appears in the query pane.

8. On the Query menu, click Display Estimated Execution Plan.

   The estimated execution plan appears in the lower pane. Notice that four index scans are used and that no table scans are used.

   Does it appear that this query's performance is affected by a lack of indexing?

   _____

▶ **To analyze the User Activity trace**

1. Switch to SQL Profiler, and then click the User Activity trace.

   Notice that all activity by your student user account appears.

   Can you determine the time that Studentxx logged on to SQL Server?

   _____

   Did the query that required the most CPU cycles take the longest duration?

   _____

   Did the query that required the most Reads take the longest duration?

   _____

Compare each of the SELECT statements captured in the trace. What is the common element in all the long-running statements that accounts for their long duration?

_____

Compare each of the long-running SELECT statements captured in the trace. What is the unique element in the long running statements that accounts for their long duration?

_____

2. Close SQL Profiler.

Exercise 3
Monitoring Locking Information with SQL Server
Enterprise Manager and Transact-SQL

In this exercise, you will open a connection to SQL Server using SQL Query Analyzer and execute a Transact-SQL script containing a BEGIN transaction statement and an UPDATE statement on a table in the Northwind database. You will then use the sp_lock system stored procedure to view the locks held by this transaction and use the sp_who system stored procedure to view the user holding the locks. You will then open a second connection to SQL Server using SQL Query Analyzer and attempt to execute an UPDATE statement on the same tables being updated by the first connection. You will then use the current activity window in SQL Server Enterprise Manager to view the blocking lock and send a message to the user of the process holding the blocking lock. Finally, you will execute a ROLLBACK TRAN statement in the first connection.

▶   **To connect to SQL Server and execute a Transact-SQL script**

1. Switch to SQL Query Analyzer.

2. On the toolbar, click the Load SQL Script button.

   A SQL Query Analyzer dialog box appears asking whether you want to save the changes to the Load.sql script.

3. Click the No button.

   The Open Query File dialog box appears.

4. Open BlockLock.sql in the C:\Labfiles\Lab 14 folder.

Note If your \Labfiles folder isn't stored on drive C, replace C:\ with the correct drive letter.

   A Transact-SQL script appears that will begin a transaction to update the ContactName for the "ANATR" CustomerID.

5. On the toolbar, click the Execute Query button to run the BlockLock.sql. script.

   Notice that the script executes and the results pane indicates that 1 row was affected.

6. In the query pane, select "EXEC sp_lock" and then click the Execute Query button on the toolbar to execute this selected phase of the script.

   Notice the information returned from the sp_lock system stored procedure. In particular, note the locks granted to the SQL Query Analyzer SPID in the Northwind database. The Northwind database has a database ID of 6. In particular, note the X in the Mode column indicating that an exclusive row lock was granted to this process.

▶ **To connect to SQL Server and execute a second Transact-SQL script**

1. On the File menu, click Connect.

   The Connect To SQL Server dialog box appears.

2. Make sure that the Windows Authentication option button is selected, and then click OK to connect to your default instance.

3. On the toolbar, click the Load SQL Script button.

   The Open Query File dialog box appears.

4. Open BlockLock2.sql in the C:\Labfiles\Lab 14 folder.

Note If your \Labfiles folder isn't stored on drive C, replace C:\ with the correct drive letter.

   A Transact-SQL script appears that will begin a transaction to update the ContactName for the "ANATR" CustomerID and then complete the transaction.

5. On the toolbar, click the Execute Query button to run the BlockLock.sql. script.

   Notice that the query does not complete its execution.

   Why is this second connection unable to complete the execution of its query?

   _____

   _____

6. Switch to the first connection in SQL Query Analyzer.

7. In the query pane, highlight **EXEC sp_lock** and then click the Execute Query button on the toolbar to execute this selected phase of the script.

   Notice the information returned from the sp_lock system stored procedure. In particular, note the locks granted to the SQL Query Analyzer SPID in the Northwind database. The Northwind database has a database ID of 6. In particular, note the Wait status listed in the Status column. The Wait status is the result of the second process's request for an exclusive lock on the row it wants to update. Notice that the Resource requested for each exclusive row lock is identical.

   Record the process ID of the process waiting for the exclusive lock. (This is displayed in the spid column.)

▶ **To view locks using the Current Activity Window in SQL Server Enterprise Manager**

1. Click the Start button, point to Programs, point to Microsoft SQL Server, and then click Enterprise Manager.

   SQL Server Enterprise Manager appears displaying the Microsoft SQL Servers and the Event Viewer (Local) console trees in the console root.

2. In the console tree, expand the Microsoft SQL Servers container, expand the SQL Server Group container, expand your default instance container, expand the Management container, expand the Current Activity container, and then click the Process Info container.

   The details pane displays information regarding all active processes.

3. In the details pane, click the row for the process ID you recorded in the previous procedure.

4. Scroll across the various columns of information available.

   Note that information is displayed regarding how long this process has been waiting for a resource (wait time is in milliseconds), the wait type, and the wait resource. Note also that the network address of the client connection is displayed.

5. In the details pane, right-click the icon for the blocking process and then click Properties.

   The Process Details – Contoso\Student*xx* – *ID* – Server*xx* dialog box appears.

   Is the last TSQL command that is displayed in the Last TSQL Command Batch pane the command that is blocking? Why or why not?

   _____

   _____

   _____

   _____

6. Click the Send Message button.

   The Send Message – Server*xx* dialog box appears.

7. In the Message text box, type **Your application is blocking. Please close your open transaction.** Then click the Send button.

   A Send Message message box appears, stating that the message was successfully sent; and a Messenger Service message box appears, containing the message. (One message box will appear behind the other message box.)

8. Click OK in each message box to close the message boxes.

9. In the Process Details – Contoso\Student*xx* – *ID* – Server*xx* dialog box, click the Close button.

▶ **To roll back the open transaction**

1. Switch to SQL Query Analyzer.

   Notice that the open transaction appears in the query pane. This is the first connection to SQL Server in which you ran the Blocklock.sql script.

2. Highlight **ROLLBACK TRAN** and then click the Execute Query button on the toolbar.

Notice that the command completed successfully.

3. Close the current connection. Do not close SQL Query Analyzer.

   The second connection appears. Notice this script has now completed successfully. Also notice that the second query does not hold any exclusive locks at the end of the transaction.

4. Close SQL Query Analyzer.

5. Switch to SQL Server Enterprise Manager.

6. In the console tree, right-click the Current Activity container and then click Refresh.

7. In the console tree, click the Locks / Process ID container.

8. In the details pane, notice that no blocking or blocked locks are held.

9. Close SQL Server Enterprise Manager.

10. Log off your computer.

Lab 12: Using SQL Server Replication

Objectives

After completing this lab, you will be able to

- Create and configure a Distributor and enable Publishers
- Create and configure publications for snapshot, transactional, and merge replication
- Create and configure push and pull subscriptions
- Monitor replication and Publication Agents, and modify their properties
- Review and modify properties of Distributors and Publishers

Before You Begin

You must successfully complete Exercises 1 and 2 in Lab 1 before you begin this lab.

Note You must log on to your student computer using the correct domain user account to have sufficient permissions to perform the lab exercises in this Lab Manual.

Estimated time to complete this lab: 75 minutes

Exercise 1
Creating and Configuring a Distributor and Enabling Publishers

In this exercise, you will configure your default instance as a Distributor and configure your partner's named instance as an enabled Publisher.

▶ **To connect to SQL Server with SQL Server Enterprise Manager**

1. Press Ctrl+Alt+Del to log on to the Contoso.msft domain.

    The Log On To Windows screen appears.

2. In the User Name text box, type **Studentxx** (where *xx* is your computer number).

3. Verify that the Log On To text box displays Contoso. (If the Log On To text box does not appear, click the Options button.)

4. In the Password text box, type **password** and then click OK.

    Personal settings are applied, and you are logged on to Microsoft Windows 2000.

5. Click Start, point to Programs, point to Microsoft SQL Server, and then click Enterprise Manager.

    SQL Server Enterprise Manager appears, displaying the Microsoft SQL Servers and the Event Viewer (Local) console trees in the console root.

6. In the console tree, expand the Microsoft SQL Servers container, expand the SQL Server Group container, expand the Serverxx\Instance2 container (your named instance), and then expand the Management container for your named instance.

7. Verify that the SQL Server Agent service for your named instance is started. If not, right-click the SQL Server Agent container and then click Start.

8. In the console tree, expand the Serverxx container (your default instance), and then expand the Management container for your default instance.

9. Verify that the SQL Server Agent service for your default instance is started. If not, right-click the SQL Server Agent container and then click Start.

▶ **To specify your default instance as a Distributor**

1. In the console tree for your default instance, right-click the Replication container and then click Configure Publishing, Subscribers, And Distribution.

    The Welcome To The Configure Publishing And Distribution Wizard screen appears.

2. Click Next.

    The Select Distributor page appears.

3. Verify that Serverxx is selected to be its own Distributor, and then click Next.

    The Specify Snapshot Folder page appears.

▶ **To create a new share and specify the snapshot folder**

1. Click the ellipsis button next to the Snapshot Folder text box.

   The Browse For Folder dialog box appears with the Repldata folder selected.

2. Right-click the Repldata folder, and then click Sharing.

   The Repldata Properties dialog box appears.

3. Click the Share This Folder option button.

4. Click the Permissions button.

   The Permissions For Repldata dialog box appears, granting Full Control permissions to the Everyone group.

5. Click the Remove button to remove Everyone from the Name list box, and then click the Add button.

   The Select Users, Computers, Or Groups dialog box appears.

6. In the lower pane, type **Contoso\SQLService** and then click the Check Names button.

   SQLService is verified.

7. In the Select Users, Computers, Or Groups dialog box, click OK.

   SQLService appears in the Name list box with the Read check box selected in the Permissions list box.

8. In the Permissions list box, select the Full Control check box for the Allow column.

9. Click OK to close the Permissions For Repldata dialog box.

10. Click OK to close the Repldata Properties dialog box.

11. In the Browse For Folder dialog box, expand My Network Places, expand Entire Network, expand Microsoft Windows Network, expand Contoso, expand Server*xx*, and then click Repldata.

12. Click OK to close the Browse For Folder dialog box.

    In the Snapshot Folder text box, \\Server*xx*\Repldata appears (replacing the default entry that uses the C$ hidden administrative share).

13. Click Next.

    A SQL Server Enterprise Manager dialog box appears, stating that SQL Server Enterprise Manager could not write to \\Server*xx*\Repldata and asking whether you still want to use this path.

    Why is SQL Server Enterprise Manager unable to write to \\Server*xx*\Repldata?

    _____

    _____

    _____

14. Click the Yes button.

The Customize The Configuration page appears, displaying the default settings that will be applied. Review the default settings.

▶ **To enable your partner's named instance as a Publisher**

1. Click the Yes, Let Me Set The Distribution Database Properties, Enable Publishers, Or Set The Publishing Settings option button, and then click Next.

The Provide Distribution Database Information page appears, displaying the default distribution database name and path. In a production environment, you would generally modify these defaults to optimize performance and provide fault tolerance.

2. Click Next.

The Enable Publishers page appears, with your default instance selected as an enabled Publisher.

3. Clear the check mark in the Server*xx* check box, select the check box for Server*yy*\Instance2 (where *yy* is your partner's computer number), and then click Next.

Note If your partner's named instance does not appear, click the New button and then register your partner's named instance using Windows authentication.

A SQL Server Enterprise Manager message box appears, stating that additional information must be provided.

4. Click the Close button.

The Publisher Properties – Server*yy*\Instance2 dialog box appears, displaying information regarding the location of the snapshot folder for this Publisher and security context information for replication agents and for the link to the Distributor.

5. In the Administrative Link To The Distributor group box, select the This Publisher Requires A Password To Establish A Link To The Distributor check box, and then click OK.

A SQL Server Enterprise Manager dialog box appears, stating that SQL Server Enterprise Manager could not write to \\Server*xx*\Repldata and asking whether you still want to use this path.

6. Click the Yes button.

In the Enable Publishers page, Server*yy*\Instance2 (your partner's named instance) appears as an enabled Publisher.

▶ **To complete the configuration of this Distributor**

1. Click Next.

The Completing The Configure Publishing And Distribution Wizard page appears.

2. Click the Finish button to configure Server*xx* as a Distributor.

   A SQL Server Enterprise Manager dialog box appears, to show the progress of the Distributor configuration.

3. When a SQL Server Enterprise Manager message box appears, stating that Server*xx* was successfully enabled as a Distributor, click OK.

   A SQL Server Enterprise Manager dialog box appears, stating that Replication Monitor has been added to the console tree.

4. Click the Close button.

▶ **To configure the distributor_admin password on the Distributor**

1. In the console tree, right-click the Replication Monitor container for your default instance, and then click Distributor Properties.

   The Publisher And Distributor Properties – Server*xx* dialog box appears with the Distributor tab selected.

2. In the Administrative Link Password group box, delete the asterisks in the Password box and then type **NewPass**.

3. In the Administrative Link Password group box, delete the asterisks in the Confirm Password box and then type **NewPass**.

4. Click OK to close the Publisher And Distributor Properties – Server*xx* dialog box.

5. Do not close SQL Server Enterprise Manager.

6. A SQL Server Enterprise Manager dialog box appears, telling you that SQL Server Enterprise Manager can automatically refresh Replication Monitor by polling the Distributor and asking whether you want to automatically refresh it.

7. Click the Yes, Automatically Refresh Replication Monitor By Polling The Distributor option button.

Note Do not continue with Exercise 2 until your partner has completed this exercise.

Exercise 2
Creating and Configuring a Transactional Publication

In this exercise, you create and configure a transactional publication, with your named instance as the Publisher and your partner's default instance as the Distributor.

▶ **To start the Create Publication wizard and select the publication and subscriber types**

1. In the SQL Server Enterprise Manager console tree, expand the Replication container for your named instance.

2. In the console tree, right-click the Publications container and then click New Publication.

   The Welcome To The Create Publication Wizard screen appears.

Note If you expand the Replication container for your default instance rather than your named instance, you will receive an error message stating that 'Server*xx*' is not enabled as a Publisher on Distributor 'Server*xx*'.

---

3. Select the Show Advanced Options In This Wizard check box, and then click Next.

   The Select Distributor page appears.

4. Click the Use The Following Server (The Selected Server Must Already Be Configured As A Distributor) option button, and then click Server*yy* (where *yy* is your partner's computer number).

5. Click Next.

   The Specify Administrative Password page appears.

6. In the Password text box, type **NewPass**.

7. In the Confirm Password text box, type **NewPass** and then click Next.

   The Choose Publication Database page appears.

8. In the Databases list box, click pubs and then click Next.

   The Select Publication Type page appears.

9. Click the Transactional Publication – Data Is Usually Updated At The Publisher, And Changes Are Sent Incrementally To Subscribers. Updates To Subscribers Preserve Transactional Consistency And Atomicity option button, and then click Next.

   The Updatable Subscriptions page appears.

10. Select both the Immediate Updating – Changes Are Immediately Applied At The Publisher Using A Two-Phase Commit Approach And Microsoft Distributed Transaction Coordinator (MS DTC) check box and the Queued Updating –

Changes Are Queued At The Subscriber Until They Can Be Applied At The Publisher check box, and then click Next.

The Specify Subscriber Types page appears.

11. Verify that only the Servers Running SQL Server 2000 check box is selected, and then click Next.

The Specify Articles page appears.

▶ **To define the publication articles and complete the create publication wizard**

1. Locate the Tables cell in the Object Type column, and then select the corresponding Publish All check box.

2. Locate the Stored Procedures cell in the Object Type column, and then select the corresponding Publish All check box.

3. Locate the Views cell in the Object Type column, and then select the corresponding Publish All check box.

Notice that tables without primary keys will not be published.

4. Click Next.

The Article Issues page appears. Review the information contained in the Issues pane and the Description pane.

5. Click Next.

The Select Publication Name And Description page appears.

6. In the Publication Name text box, type **PubsReplicate** and then click Next.

The Customize The Properties Of The Publication page appears. Review the default values for the remaining properties of this publication.

7. Verify that the No, Create The Publication As Specified option button is selected, review the publication properties, and then click Next.

The Completing The Create Publication Wizard screen appears.

8. Click the Finish button to create the publication.

A SQL Server Enterprise Manager dialog box appears, displaying the progress of the publication being created.

9. When a second SQL Server Enterprise Manager dialog box appears, stating that the publication was successfully created, click the Close button.

The PubsReplicate:pubs publication appears in the details pane for the Publications container of your named instance, displaying the publication type Transactional.

10. Do not close SQL Server Enterprise Manager.

Exercise 3
Creating and Configuring a Merge Publication

In this exercise, you will create and configure a merge transactional replication, with your named instance as the Publisher and your partner's default instance as the Distributor.

▶ **To start the Create Publication wizard and select the publication and subscriber types**

1. In the SQL Server Enterprise Manager console tree, expand the Replication container for your named instance.

2. In the console tree, right-click the Publications container and then click New Publication.

   The Welcome To The Create Publication Wizard screen appears.

3. Select the Show Advanced Options In This Wizard check box, and then click Next.

   The Choose Publication Database page appears.

4. In the Databases list box, click Northwind and then click Next.

   The Select Publication Type page appears.

5. Click the Merge Publication – Data Can Be Updated At The Publisher Or Any Subscriber. Changes Are Merged Periodically At The Publisher. This Supports Mobile, Occasionally Connected Subscribers option button, and then click Next.

   The Specify Subscriber Types page appears.

6. Verify that only the Servers Running SQL Server 2000 check box is selected, and then click Next.

   The Specify Articles page appears.

▶ **To define the publication articles and complete the Create Publication wizard**

1. Click the Article Defaults button.

   The Default Article Type dialog box appears.

2. Verify that Table Articles is selected, and then click OK.

   The Default Table Article Properties dialog box appears with the General tab selected.

3. Click the Resolver tab.

4. Select the Allow Subscribers To Resolve Conflicts Interactively During On-Demand Synchronization check box, and then click OK.

   The Specify Articles dialog box reappears.

5. Locate the Tables cell in the Object Type column, and then select the corresponding Publish All check box.

6. Locate the Stored Procedures cell in the Object Type column, and then select the corresponding Publish All check box.

7. Locate the Views cell in the Object Type column, and then select the corresponding Publish All check box.

8. Locate the User Defined Functions cell in the Object Type column, and then select the corresponding Publish All check box.

9. Click Next.

The Article Issues page appears. Review the information contained in the Issues pane and the Description pane.

10. Click Next.

The Select Publication Name And Description page appears.

11. In the Publication Name text box, type **NorthwindSales** and then click Next.

The Customize The Properties Of The Publication page appears. Review the default values for the remaining properties of this publication.

Note Do not continue any further with the Create Publication wizard at this time. We will return to the wizard after a script has been executed in SQL Query Analyzer.

▶ **To create a user-defined function (UDF) to use for a static filter**

1. Click Start, point to Programs, point to Microsoft SQL Server, and then click Query Analyzer.

The Connect To SQL Server dialog box appears.

2. Click the ellipsis button next to the SQL Server drop-down combo box.

The Select Server dialog box appears.

3. In the Active Servers list box, click Server*xx*\Instance2 and then click OK.

4. Ensure that the Windows Authentication option button is selected, and then click OK to connect to the named instance on Server*xx*.

5. On the toolbar, click the Load SQL Script button.

The Open Query File dialog box appears.

6. Open the UDF.sql file in C:\Labfiles\Lab 15.

Note If your \Labfiles folder isn't stored on drive C, replace C:\ with the correct drive letter.

The script creates a user-defined function to return rows based on the week number.

7. On the toolbar, click the Execute Query button.

   The script creates the UDF user-defined function.

8. After the script executes successfully, close SQL Query Analyzer to return to the Create Publication wizard.

► **To define a filter and complete the NorthwindSales publication**

1. Click the Yes, I Will Define Data Filters, Enable Anonymous Subscriptions, Or Customize Other Properties option button and then click Next.

   The Filter Data page appears.

2. Select the Horizontally, By Filtering The Rows Of Published Data check box and then click Next.

   The Enable Dynamic Filters page appears.

3. Verify that the No, Use Static Filters option button is selected, and then click Next.

   The Generate Filters Automatically page appears.

4. In the Table To Filter drop-down list, click [dbo].[Orders].

5. In the text box, complete the WHERE clause in the SELECT statement by typing **dbo.udf_wknum(orderdate) between 1 and 12** and then click Next.

   A SQL Server Enterprise Manager dialog box appears, to display the progress of the filters being generated for the publication. When the filters have been created, the Filter Table Rows page appears. Notice this static filter limits the rows in the Orders table. Also notice that you can extend the filtering by defining a join between the filtered table and a related table.

6. Click Next.

   The Optimize Synchronization page appears.

7. Click the Yes, Minimize The Amount Of Data option button, and then click Next.

   The Allow Anonymous Subscriptions page appears.

8. Verify that the No, Allow Only Named Subscriptions option button is selected, and then click Next.

   The Set Snapshot Agent Schedule page appears.

9. Verify that the Create The First Snapshot Immediately check box is selected, and then click Next.

   The Completing The Create Publication Wizard screen appears. Review the properties of the publication you are about to create.

10. Click the Finish button to create the publication.

    A SQL Server Enterprise Manager dialog box appears, displaying the progress of the publication being created.

11. When a second SQL Server Enterprise Manager dialog box appears, stating that the publication was successfully created, click the Close button.

    The NorthwindSales:Northwind publication appears in the details pane for the Publications container for your named instance, displaying a type of Merge.

12. Do not close SQL Server Enterprise Manager.

Exercise 4
Creating and Configuring a Push Subscription

In this exercise, you will create and configure a push subscription to your PubsReplicate:pubs publication with your partner's named instance as the Subscriber.

▶ **To start the Push Subscription wizard, select the Subscriber, specify the destination database, and specify the agent location**

1. In the details pane for the Publications container for your named instance, right-click PubsReplicate:pubs and then click Push New Subscription.

   The Welcome To The Push Subscription Wizard screen appears.

2. Select the Show Advanced Options In This Wizard check box, and then click Next.

   The Choose Subscribers page appears.

3. In the Subscribers list box, click Server*yy*\Instance2 (where *yy* is your partner's computer number) and then click Next.

   The Choose Destination Database page appears.

4. Click the Browse Or Create button.

   The Browse Databases On 'Server*yy*\Instance2' dialog box appears, displaying each of the existing databases on your partner's named instance.

5. Click the Create New button.

   The Database Properties - dialog box appears.

6. In the Name text box, type **PubsReplica** and then click OK to create the new database using default values.

7. In the Browse Databases On 'Server*yy*\Instance2' dialog box, verify that PubsReplica is selected and then click OK.

8. In the Choose Destination Database page, click Next.

   The Set Distribution Agent Location page appears.

9. Verify that the Run The Agent At The Distributor option button is selected, and then click Next.

   The Set Distribution Agent Schedule page appears.

▶ **To configure the push subscription schedule, start the Snapshot Agent, and complete the Push Subscription wizard**

1. Verify that the Continuously – Provides Minimal Latency Between When An Action Occurs At The Publisher And Is Propagated To The Subscriber option button is selected, and then click Next.

   The Initialize Subscription page appears.

2. Verify that the Yes, Initialize The Schema And Data option button is selected.

3. Select the Start The Snapshot Agent To Begin The Initialization Process Immediately check box, and then click Next.

   The Updatable Subscriptions page appears.

4. Click the Immediate Updating With Queued Updating As A Standby In Case Of Failure option button, and then click Next.

   The Start Required Services page appears. Notice that the SQL Server Agent service on Serveryy is required along with the MS DTC service on both Serverxx and Serveryy.

   Why is the SQL Server Agent service required only on Serveryy?

   _____

   _____

   _____

5. In the grid, verify that the check box for each listed service is selected and then click Next.

   The Completing The Push Subscription Wizard screen appears. Review the properties of the push subscription you are about to create.

6. Click the Finish button.

   A SQL Server Enterprise Manager dialog box appears, showing the progress of the push subscription being created.

   A second SQL Server Enterprise Manager dialog box appears, stating that the subscription was successfully created. It also states that neither the SQL Server Agent service on your partner's default instance nor the MS DTC service on your partner's named instance could be started because access was denied.

   Why was access denied?

   _____

   _____

   _____

   Will the Distribution Agent have access to the snapshot folder? Why or why not?

   _____

   _____

   _____

   Will the Distribution Agent have access to the distribution database on the Distributor and the destination database on the Subscriber? Why or why not?

   _____

   _____

   _____

7. Click the Close button.

Note Before you continue, verify with your partner that the SQL Server Agent service for your partner's default instance is running. Also, verify that the MS DTC service on your partner's server is running.

8. Do not close SQL Server Enterprise Manager.

Exercise 5
Creating and Configuring a Pull Subscription

In this exercise, you will create and configure a pull subscription to your partner's NorthwindSales publication using your named instance as the Subscriber.

▶ **To start the Pull Subscription wizard, select the publication, and specify the destination database**

1. In the SQL Server Enterprise Manager console tree, expand the Replication container for your named instance.

2. Right-click the Subscriptions container, and then click New Pull Subscription.

   The Welcome To The Pull Subscription Wizard screen appears.

3. Select the Show Advanced Options In This Wizard check box, and then click Next.

   The Look For Publications page appears.

4. Verify that the Look At Publications From Registered Servers option button is selected, and then click Next.

   The Choose Publication page appears.

5. Expand Serveryy\Instance2, click NorthwindSales:Northwind, and then click Next.

   The Choose Destination Database page appears.

Note If you cannot expand Serveryy\Instance2 and click NorthwindSales: Northwind, close SQL Server Enterprise Manager, reopen it, and then start this exercise again.

---

6. Click the New button.

   The Database Properties - dialog box appears.

7. In the Name text box, type **NWindSales** and then click OK.

   The NWindSales database is created using default parameters.

8. In the Choose Destination Database page, verify that NWindSales is selected and then click Next.

   The Initialize Subscription page appears.

▶ **To configure the remaining pull subscription properties and complete the Pull Subscription wizard**

1. Verify that the Yes, Initialize The Schema And Data option button is selected.

2. Select the Start The Merge Agent To Initialize The Subscription Immediately check box, and then click Next.

   The Snapshot Delivery page appears.

3. Verify that the Use Snapshot Files From The Default Snapshot Folder For This Publication option button is selected, and then click Next.

   The Set Merge Agent Schedule page appears.

4. Click the On Demand Only – You Can Synchronize This Subscription Using SQL Server Enterprise Manager Or The Windows Synchronization Manager option button, and then click Next.

   The Set Subscription Priority page appears.

5. Verify that the Use The Publisher As A Proxy For The Subscriber When Resolving Conflicts option button is selected, and then click Next.

   The Completing The Pull Subscription Wizard screen appears. Review the properties of the pull subscription about to be created.

6. Click the Finish button.

   A SQL Server Enterprise Manager dialog box appears, displaying the progress of the pull subscription being created.

7. When a SQL Server Enterprise Manager message box appears, stating that the pull subscription was created successfully, click OK.

8. Do not close SQL Server Enterprise Manager.

Exercise 6
Monitoring Replication

In this exercise, you will configure Replication Monitor settings and then verify that the initial snapshots were successfully created. This includes viewing the execution history of one of the Snapshot Agents and its profile. You will then verify which additional replication agents have run. Finally, you will change a record in the pubs database in your named instance and verify that the change is replicated to the PubsReplica database in your partner's named instance.

▶ **To configure Replication Monitor settings**

1. In the SQL Server Enterprise Manager console tree, expand your default instance container and then expand the Replication Monitor container for your default instance.

   A SQL Server Enterprise Manager dialog box appears.

2. Click the Yes, Automatically Refresh Replication Monitor By Polling The Distributor option button.

3. Click the Set Refresh Rate button.

   The Refresh Rate And Settings dialog box appears.

4. In the Refresh Results Pane group box, change the value in the spin box to 3.

5. Click OK.

▶ **To verify that the initial snapshots were created, view the execution history and the Snapshot Agent profile**

1. In the console tree, expand the Agents container and then click the Snapshot Agents container.

   The Snapshot Agents for each publication appear in the details pane. Notice that the status column for each Snapshot Agent indicates success. Notice also that the Last Action column indicates that the snapshot was successfully generated.

2. In the details pane, right-click NorthwindSales and then click Agent History.

   The Snapshot Agent History dialog box appears, providing information regarding the snapshot jobs that have executed.

3. Click the Session Details button.

   The Latest History Of Snapshot Agent dialog box appears. In the list box, notice the steps taken to create the snapshot files.

4. Click the Close button.

5. In the Snapshot Agent History dialog box, click the Agent Profile button.

   The Snapshot Agent Profiles dialog box appears.

6. Click the View Details button.

The Replication Agent Profile Details dialog box appears. Notice the default parameters for the Snapshot Agent.

7. Click the Close button to close the Replication Agent Profile Details dialog box.

8. Click OK to close the Snapshot Agent Profiles dialog box.

▶ **To verify which additional replication agents have run**

1. In the console tree (in the Replication Monitor container for your default instance), expand Publishers, expand your partner's named instance, and then click NorthwindSales:Northwind (your merge publication).

The replication agent for this merge publication appears in the details pane. Notice that only the Snapshot Agent has run. The Distribution Agent indicates that it has never started.

2. In the console tree, click PubReplicate:pubs (your transactional publication).

The replication agent for this transactional publication appears in the details pane. Notice that the Snapshot Agent has run, and that each of the other agents is idle because no replicated transactions are available to replicate and because no queued transactions are available.

▶ **To update the pubs database in your named instance and verify that the change is replicated to the PubsReplica database in your partner's named instance**

1. In the console tree, click your named instance container.

2. On the Tools menu, click SQL Query Analyzer.

You are connected to your named instance as Contoso\Student*xx*.

3. On the toolbar, click the Load SQL Script button.

The Open Query File dialog box appears.

4. Open PubsUpdate.sql in the C:\Labfiles\Lab 15 folder.

Note If your \Labfiles folder isn't stored on drive C, replace C:\ with the correct drive letter.

A Transact-SQL script appears that contains an UPDATE statement that updates the last name of the author, Johnson White, to Johnson Black in the pubs database.

Note Do not continue until you and your partner can execute the following steps synchronously.

---

5. On the toolbar, click the Execute Query button.

The script is executed, and one record is updated.

6. Switch to SQL Server Enterprise Manager.

7. In the console tree, expand your default instance container, expand the Replication Monitor container, expand the Publishers container, expand Server*yy*\Instance2, and then click PubsReplicate:pubs (your transactional publication).

8. In the details pane, observe the Log Reader Agent and the Distribution Agent (named Server*xx*\Instance2:PubsReplica). After about 10 seconds, each of these agents will run and update the PubsReplica database on your partner's named instance. Each agent will indicate that one transaction with two commands was delivered. After about 10 more seconds, these agents will indicate that no replicated transactions are currently available.

9. Switch to SQL Query Analyzer.

10. In the query pane, highlight the following query.

```
SELECT * FROM PubsReplica.dbo.authors WHERE au_lname = 'Black'
```

11. On the toolbar, click the Execute Query button.

The replicated change from the pubs database on your partner's named instance has been replicated to the PubsReplica database on your named instance.

12. Do not close SQL Server Enterprise Manager or SQL Query Analyzer.

Exercise 7
Resolving Conflicts Interactively

In this exercise, you and your partner will each execute a Transact-SQL script that updates an employee record in the Employees table in the Northwind database in your named instance. Next, you will each execute a Transact-SQL script that updates the same employee record in the Employee table in the NorthwindSales database in your named instance. Then you and your partner will each configure your pull subscription using Windows Synchronization Manager to enable interactive conflict resolution. Finally, you and your partner will each use Windows Synchronization Manager to synchronize the Northwind database on your partner's named instance with the NwindSales database on your named instance.

▶ **To update a record in the Employees table in the Northwind database in your named instance**

1. On the SQL Query Analyzer toolbar, click the Load SQL Script button.

   The Open Query File dialog box appears.

2. Open NorthwindUpdate.sql in the C:\Labfiles\Lab 15 folder.

Note If your \Labfiles folder isn't stored on drive C, replace C:\ with the correct drive letter.

This script updates Employee ID 1, changing the last name and title.

3. On the toolbar, click the Execute Query button.

   One record is updated.

▶ **To update a record in the Employees table in the NwindSales database**

1. On the SQL Query Analyzer toolbar, click the Load SQL Script button.

   The Open Query File dialog box appears.

2. Open NwindPullUpdate.sql in the C:\Labfiles\Lab 15 folder.

Note If your \Labfiles folder isn't stored on drive C, replace C:\ with the correct drive letter.

This script updates Employee ID 1, changing the last name and title. Notice that the last name and title for this employee are different from the script in the previous procedure.

3. On the toolbar, click the Execute Query button.

   One record is updated.

▶ **To configure the pull subscription to the NorthwindSales:Northwind publication to resolve conflict interactively**

1. Click Start, point to Programs, point to Accessories, and then click Synchronize.

   The Items To Synchronize dialog box appears.

2. Click NwindSales:NorthwindSales (Server*xx*\Instance2), and then click the Properties button.

   The SQL Server Subscription Properties dialog box appears with the Identification tab selected.

3. Click the Other tab.

4. Click the Resolve Conflicts Interactively (Only Applies To Articles That Support Interactive Resolution) option button, and then click OK.

   A Microsoft SQL Server 2000 dialog box appears, asking whether you are sure you want to change the conflict resolution mode.

5. Click the Yes button.

Note Do not continue until you and your partner execute the following steps synchronously.

▶ **To manually initiate synchronization with your partner's Northwind database and resolve the conflict interactively**

1. Clear the My Current Home Page check box.

2. Verify that the NwindSales:NorthwindSales (Server*xx*\Instance2) check box is selected, and then click the Synchronize button.

   The Synchronizing dialog box appears. After a few moments, the Microsoft Replication Conflict Viewer for 'Northwind' – '[dbo].[Employees]' dialog box appears. Notice that the update that occurred at the Publisher is the suggested resolution.

3. Click the Resolve With This Data option button.

   The synchronization process completes.

4. Switch to SQL Query Analyzer.

5. On the toolbar, click the Clear Window button.

6. In the query pane, type the following query.

```
SELECT * FROM NwindSales.dbo.Employees WHERE EmployeeID = 1
```

7. On the toolbar, click the Execute Query button.

   Notice that the resolved data has been replicated from the Northwind database in your partner's named instance to the NwindSales database in your named instance.

8. Close SQL Server Enterprise Manager and SQL Query Analyzer. Do not save any changes.

9. Log off your computer.

Lab 13: Implementing Log Shipping

Objectives

After completing this lab, you will be able to

- Automate log shipping using the Database Maintenance Plan wizard
- Monitor log shipping
- Promote a standby server to become the primary server

Before You Begin

You must successfully complete Exercises 1 and 2 in Lab 1 before you begin this lab.

Note You must log on to your student computer using the correct domain user account to have sufficient permissions to perform the lab exercises in this Lab Manual.

Estimated time to complete this lab: 30 minutes

Exercise 1
Configuring a Standby Server

In this exercise, you will automate log shipping using the Database Maintenance Planner wizard in Microsoft SQL Server Enterprise Manager. You will use your partner's named instance as the standby server, and your partner will use your named instance.

▶ **To connect to SQL Server with SQL Server Enterprise Manager**

1. Press Ctrl+Alt+Del to log on to the Contoso.msft domain.

   The Log On To Windows screen appears.

2. In the User Name text box, type **Studentxx** (where *xx* is your computer number).

3. Verify that the Log On To text box displays Contoso. (If the Log On To text box does not appear, click the Options button.)

4. In the Password text box, type **password** and then click OK.

   Personal settings are applied, and you are logged on to Microsoft Windows 2000.

5. Click Start, point to Programs, point to Microsoft SQL Server, and then click Enterprise Manager.

   SQL Server Enterprise Manager appears displaying the Microsoft SQL Servers and the Event Viewer (Local) console trees in the console root.

6. In the console tree, expand the Microsoft SQL Servers container, expand the SQL Server Group container, expand the Serverxx\Instance2 container (your named instance), and then expand the Management container for your named instance.

7. Verify that the SQL Server Agent service for the named instance is started. If not, right-click the SQL Server Agent container and then click Start.

8. In the console tree, expand the Serverxx container (your default instance), and then expand the Management container for your default instance.

9. Verify that the SQL Server Agent service for the default instance is started. If not, right-click the SQL Server Agent container and then click Start.

▶ **To attach a database**

1. In the console tree, expand the Databases container for your default instance.

2. Right-click the Databases container, point to All Tasks, and then click Attach Database.

   The Attach Database – Serverxx dialog box appears.

3. Click the ellipsis button to browse for the LogShipDB.mdf file.

   The Browse for Existing File – Serverxx dialog box appears.

4. Click LogShipDB.mdf in C:\Labfiles\Lab 16, and then click OK.

Note If your \Labfiles folder isn't stored on drive C, replace C:\ with the correct drive letter.

The Attach Database – Server*xx* dialog box appears. Notice that the LogShipDB database is about to be attached.

5. In the Specify Database Owner drop-down box, click sa.

6. Click OK to attach the LogShipDB database.

A SQL Server Enterprise Manager message box appears informing you that the attachment of the database has completed successfully.

7. Click OK.

Notice that the LogShipDB database appears in the list of databases.

▶ **To configure shares for use in log shipping**

1. Open Windows Explorer, and browse to C:\Program Files\Microsoft SQL Server\Mssql.

Note If your SQL Server 2000 default instance is not installed on drive C, replace C:\ with the correct drive letter.

2. Right-click the Backup folder, and then click Sharing.

The Backup Properties dialog box appears.

3. Click the Share This Folder option button, change the share name to **Server*xx*LogBackups** (where *xx* is your computer number) in the Share Name text box, and then click OK.

What users will have access to read and write files to C:\Program Files\Microsoft SQL Server\Mssql through this shared folder?

_____

_____

_____

4. Browse to C:\Program Files\Microsoft SQL Server\Mssql$Instance2.

Note If your SQL Server 2000 named instance is not installed on drive C, replace C:\ with the correct drive letter.

5. Right-click the Backup folder, and then click Sharing.

The Backup Properties dialog box appears.

6. Click the Share This Folder option button, change the name to **NewPrimaryLogBackups** in the Share Name text box, and then click OK.

What users will have access to read and write files to C:\Program Files\Microsoft SQL Server\Mssql$Instance2 through this shared folder?

_____

_____

_____

Note Do not continue until your partner has completed this procedure.

---

7. Close Windows Explorer.

▶ **To start the Database Maintenance Plan wizard and define the primary server for log shipping**

1. In the console tree, right-click the LogShipDB container in the Databases container for your default instance, point to All Tasks, and then click Maintenance Plan.

   The Welcome To The Database Maintenance Plan Wizard page appears.

2. Click Next.

   The Select Servers page appears.

3. Select the (Local) check box, and then click Next.

   The Select Databases page appears with the LogShipDB check box selected.

4. Verify that the These Databases option button is selected, select the Ship The Transaction Logs To Other SQL Servers (Log Shipping) check box, and then click Next.

   The Update Data Optimization Information page appears. No options are selected.

5. Click Next.

   The Database Integrity Check page appears. No options are selected.

6. Click Next.

   The Specify The Database Backup Plan page appears.

7. Clear the Back Up The Database As Part Of The Maintenance Plan check box, and then click Next.

   The Specify Transaction Log Backup Disk Directory page appears.

8. Verify that the Use The Default Backup Directory option button is selected.

9. Select the Remove Files Older Than check box, and then select 15 in the spin box and Minutes in the drop-down list.

10. Click Next.

    The Specify The Transaction Log Share page appears.

11. In the Network Share Name For Backup Directory text box, type **\\Serverxx\ServerxxLogBackups** (where *xx* is your computer number) and then click Next.

   The wizard verifies that the specified share exists, and the Specify The Log Shipping Destinations page appears.

▶ **To configure the destination server**

1. Click the Add button.

   The Add Destination Database dialog box appears.

2. In the Server Name drop-down list, click Serveryy\Instance2 (where *yy* is your partner's computer number). Notice the default properties for the destination database.

3. In the Database Load State group box, click the Standby Mode option button and then select the Terminate Users In Database (Recommended) check box.

4. Select the Allow Database To Assume Primary Role check box.

5. In the Directory text box, type **\\Serveryy\NewPrimaryLogBackups** (where *yy* is your partner's computer number) and then click OK.

   The wizard attempts to verify access through the share.

   A SQL Server Enterprise Manager dialog box appears stating that SQL Server Enterprise Manager cannot verify that this is a valid share, and asking whether you wish to continue anyway.

   Why is SQL Server Enterprise Manager unable to verify that this is a valid share?

   _____

   _____

   _____

6. Click the Yes button. Use the share anyway.

   The Specify The Log Shipping Destinations page reappears displaying the destination server and database.

7. Click Next.

   The Initialize The Destination Databases page appears.

8. Verify that the Perform A Full Database Backup Now option button is selected, and then click Next.

   The Log Shipping Schedules page appears.

▶ **To define the log shipping schedules**

1. Click the Change button to modify the backup schedule.

   The Edit Recurring Job Schedule dialog box appears.

2. In the Daily Frequency group box, change the Occurs Every spin box from 15 minutes to 1 minute and then click OK.

   The Log Shipping Schedules page reappears.

3. Change the Copy/Load Frequency spin box from 15 minutes to 1 minute.

4. Change the File Retention Period spin box from 24 hours to 1 hour.

5. Click Next.

   The Log Shipping Thresholds page appears. Notice that the Backup Alert Threshold is set to 5 minutes and the Out Of Sync Alert Threshold is set to 3 minutes.

6. Click Next.

   The Specify The Log Shipping Monitor Server Information page appears.

7. In the SQL Server drop-down list, click Server*yy* (where *yy* is your partner's computer number). This simulates using a third server for the monitoring server.

8. Verify that the Use Windows Authentication option button is selected, and then click Next.

   The Reports To Generate page appears.

9. Select the Send E-Mail Report To Operator check box, and then select Student*xx* in the drop-down list.

10. Click Next.

    The Maintenance Plan History page appears.

11. Click Next.

    The Database Maintenance Plan Wizard Summary page appears.

12. In the Plan Name text box, type **Log Shipping** and then click Next.

    The Completing The Database Maintenance Plan Wizard page appears.

13. Click the Finish button.

    Notice the progress of the steps the wizard is performing. When the maintenance plan completes, a Database Maintenance Plan Wizard message box appears informing you that the maintenance plan was successfully created.

14. Click OK to acknowledge the Database Maintenance Plan Wizard message box.

▶ **To verify the read-only copy of your partner's LogShipDB database**

1. In the console tree, expand your partner's named instance, and then expand your partner's Databases container.

2. Click the Databases container and then, on the toolbar, click the Refresh button.

   In the Databases container for Server*yy*\Instance2, the LogShipDB database container appears containing a read-only copy of the LogShipDB database. If it does not appear, right-click the Databases container and then click Refresh.

Note Do not continue until your partner's read-only copy of the LogShipDB database appears in your named instance container.

3. Don't close SQL Server Enterprise Manager.

Exercise 2
Monitoring a Log-Shipping Pair

In this exercise, you will monitor log shipping using the Log Shipping Monitor in SQL Server Enterprise Manager. You will use your default instance to monitor your partner's default instance and your named instance.

▶ **To view your partner's log shipping pair using Log Shipping Monitor**

1. In the SQL Server Enterprise Manager console tree, expand your default instance container, and then expand the Management container.

2. Click the Management container and then, on the toolbar, click the Refresh button.

   The Log Shipping Monitor appears in the Management container of your default instance.

3. In the Management container, click Log Shipping Monitor.

   The current status of your partner's log shipping pair is displayed in the details pane.

4. On the toolbar, click the Show/Hide Console Tree/Favorites button.

   Notice that the window now displays only the contents of the details pane (for easier viewing of all columns).

5. Resize the displayed columns, and verify the status of the log shipping pair. If your partner configured log shipping properly, the status column indicates that the log shipping pair is in sync.

▶ **To view the log shipping execution history information**

1. Right-click the log shipping pair, and then click View Backup History.

   The Database Maintenance Plan History – Server*yy* dialog box appears (where *yy* is your partner's computer number) displaying the history of your partner's Log Shipping maintenance plan. Notice that the transaction log is being backed up every minute and each successful job has a blue check mark in the Status column.

2. In the Status drop-down list, click Failed.

   Any failed backup jobs are displayed.

3. Click the Close button.

4. Right-click the log shipping pair, and then click View Copy/Restore History.

   The Secondary Server Log Shipping History – Server*yy*\Instance2 dialog box appears. Notice that the copy job and the load job occur every minute. The load job restores all transaction log backup files that have been copied, and then the copy job connects to the primary server and copies any new transaction log backup files to the standby server.

5. Click the Close button.

6. Right-click your partner's log shipping pair, and then click Properties.

   The Log Shipping Pair Properties dialog box appears. Notice, in the Last File Loaded group box, that the Load Delta indicates that the synchronization delay between the primary database and the standby database is 1 minute.

7. Click OK to close the Log Shipping Pair Properties dialog box.

8. On the toolbar, click the Show/Hide Console Tree/Favorites button.

   Notice that the window now displays the contents of the console tree and the details pane.

9. Do not close SQL Server Enterprise Manager.

Exercise 3
Promoting a Standby Server

In this exercise, you will open SQL Query Analyzer and update a record in the LogShipDB database. You will then promote the standby server to primary and verify that the updated record appears on the new primary server.

▶ **To update a record in the LogShipDB database**

1. On the SQL Server Enterprise Manager Tools menu, click SQL Query Analyzer.

   You are connected to your default instance of SQL Server.

2. On the toolbar, click the Load SQL Script button.

   The Open Query File dialog box appears.

3. Open LogShipChangeData.sql in the C:\Labfiles\Lab 16 folder.

Note If your \Labfiles folder isn't stored on drive C, replace C:\ with the correct drive letter.

   Notice that this script changes the ContactTitle field for one of the customers in the LogShipDB database.

4. On the toolbar, click the Execute Query button to execute the script.

   Notice that the ContactTitle field for CustomerID ANATR is changed from "Owner" to "Owner_Changed".

5. Do not close SQL Query Analyzer.

▶ **To demote the primary server and disable the log copy and log restore jobs on the standby server**

1. On the toolbar, click the Load SQL Script button.

   The Open Query File dialog box appears.

2. Open DemotePrimary.sql in the C:\Labfiles\Lab 16 folder.

Note If your \Labfiles folder isn't stored on drive C, replace C:\ with the correct drive letter.

   This script runs the sp_change_primary_role system stored procedure, which backs up the current transaction log for the LogShipDB database and sets the database to Read-Only.

3. In the toolbar, click the Execute Query button to execute the DemotePrimary.sql script.

Note You might receive a message box stating that the database is in the middle of a restore. If you receive this message box, the script cannot be executed for a few seconds. Wait for a few seconds, and then try to execute the script again.

The script executes and displays a message regarding the backup of the current transaction log.

Note If the current transaction log is empty, you will receive only a message stating that the command completed successfully.

---

4. Switch to SQL Server Enterprise Manager.

5. Expand your partner's named instance container, expand the Management container, expand the SQL Server Agent container, and then click the Jobs container.

   The current jobs are displayed in the details pane, including two log shipping jobs.

6. In the details pane, right-click the Log Shipping Copy For Server*xx*.LogShipDB_Logshipping job and then click Disable Job.

7. In the details pane, right-click the Log Shipping Restore For Server*xx*.LogShipDB_Logshipping job and then click Disable Job.

▶ **To promote the standby server**

1. Switch to SQL Query Analyzer.

2. On the File menu, click Connect.

   The Connect To SQL Server dialog box appears.

3. Next to the SQL Server drop-down list, click the ellipsis button.

   The Select Server dialog box appears.

4. Click Server*yy*\Instance2 (where *yy* is your partner's computer number), and then click OK.

5. Verify that the Windows Authentication option button is selected, and then click OK.

   You are connected to your partner's named instance.

6. On the toolbar, click the Load SQL Script button.

   The Open Query File dialog box appears.

7. Open PromoteSecondary.sql in the C:\Labfiles\Lab 16 folder.

Note If your \Labfiles folder isn't stored on drive C, replace C:\ with the correct drive letter.

This script runs the sp_change_secondary_role system stored procedure, which copies the current transaction log from the primary server and restores it to the LogShipDB database on the standby server. It also restores the database to multiuser mode and removes the Read-Only setting.

8. On the toolbar, click the Execute Query button to execute the PromoteSecondary.sql script.

Notice that the script copies the current transaction log (and any other logs it has not previously copied) and applies it to the database on the standby server. It deletes the copy and load jobs that were running on the former standby server and enables the transaction log backup job on the new primary server. If the second result set indicates that exclusive control of the database could not be obtained to perform the restore task, rerun the system stored procedure.

▶ **To update the monitor server for your log shipping pair and verify the update was copied**

1. On the File menu, click Connect.

   The Connect To SQL Server dialog box appears.

2. Next to the SQL Server drop-down list, click the ellipsis button.

   The Select Server dialog box appears.

3. Click Server*yy* (where *yy* is your partner's computer number), and then click OK.

4. Verify that the Windows Authentication option button is selected, and then click OK.

   You are connected to your partner's default instance.

5. On the toolbar, click the Load SQL Script button.

   The Open Query File dialog box appears.

6. Open UpdateMonitorServer.sql in the C:\Labfiles\Lab 16 folder.

Note If your \Labfiles folder isn't stored on drive C, replace C:\ with the correct drive letter.

This script runs the sp_change_monitor_role system stored procedure, updating the monitor server regarding the change in the role of the primary and standby servers. It also specifies the storage location for the transaction log backup files being created on the new primary (former standby) server.

7. In the UpdateMonitorServer.sql script, replace the *xx* variable with your computer number and the *yy* variable with your partner's computer number.

8. On the toolbar, click the Execute Query button to execute the UpdateMonitorServer.sql script.

   The command executes successfully.

9. Switch to the SQL query pane containing the connection to Server*yy*\Instance2.

10. On the toolbar, click the Clear Window button.

11. In the query pane, type **SELECT * FROM LogShipDB.dbo.Customers WHERE CustomerID = 'ANATR'** and then click the Execute Query button on the toolbar.

Notice that the ContactTitle change from "Owner" to "Owner_Changed" appears in the new primary server.

12. On the toolbar, click the Clear Window button.

13. In the query pane, type **UPDATE LogShipDB.dbo.Customers SET ContactTitle = 'Owner' WHERE CustomerID = 'ANATR'** and then click the Execute Query button on the toolbar.

    Notice that the query executes successfully. The new primary database is functioning successfully. If you receive an error stating that BEGIN TRANS-ACTION could not run because the database is read-only, you are connected to the default instance rather than the named instance.

14. Switch to SQL Server Enterprise Manager.

15. In the console tree, expand your partner's named instance container, expand the Management container, expand the SQL Server Agent container, and then click the Jobs container.

    The jobs appear in the details pane.

16. In the console tree, right-click the Jobs container and then click Refresh.

17. In the details pane, right-click the Transaction Log Backup Job For DB Maintenance Plan 'Log Shipping' job and then click View Job History.

    The Job History – Server*yy*\Instance2 dialog box appears. Notice that this job is now backing up the transaction log for the new primary server (Server*yy*\Instance2).

18. Click the Close button to close the Job History – Server*yy*\Instance2 dialog box.

19. In the console tree, expand your default instance, expand the Management container, and then click the Database Maintenance Plans container.

    The Log Shipping maintenance plan appears in the details pane.

20. In the details pane, right-click Log Shipping and then click Maintenance Plan History.

    The Database Maintenance Plan History – Server*xx* dialog box appears displaying the same backup transaction log job history as step 17.

21. Click the Close button.

22. Close SQL Server Enterprise Manager and SQL Query Analyzer. Do not save any changes.

23. Log off of your computer.